On the cover:

Mute swans are large white birds that look quite different when they are born. At birth, the baby swans, called chicks, are brownish gray. Slowly, over the next 12 months, the chicks turn white. Mute swans are silent most of the time. When frightened, they will hiss and grunt. Unlike many other water birds, mute swans do not dive. Instead they plunge their head and neck below the water's surface to find food.

California Treasures

A Reading/Language Arts Program

Program Authors

Diane August
Donald R. Bear
Janice A. Dole
Jana Echevarria
Douglas Fisher
David Francis
Vicki Gibson
Jan E. Hasbrouck
Scott G. Paris
Timothy Shanahan
Josefina V. Tinajero

Macmillan/McGraw-Hill

Contributors

Time Magazine, Accelerated Reader

Students with print disabilities may be eligible to obtain an accessible, audio version of the pupil edition of this textbook. Please call Recording for the Blind & Dyslexic at 1-800-221-4792 for complete information.

B

The McGraw·Hill Companies

Macmillan/McGraw-Hill

Published by Macmillan/McGraw-Hill, of McGraw-Hill Education, a division of The McGraw-Hill Companies, Inc., Two Penn Plaza, New York, New York 10121.

Printed in the United States of America

ISBN: 978-0-02-199967-5/2, Bk. 2
MHID: 0-02-199967-8/2, Bk. 2
8 9 (RJE/LEH) 12

Welcome to
California *Treasures*

Imagine seeing a hailstone as big as a baseball, learning about what an inventor could do with peanuts, or reading about cows that type. Your **Student Book** contains these and other award-winning fiction and nonfiction selections.

Treasures Meets California Standards

The instruction provided with each reading selection in your **Student Book** will ensure that you meet all the **California Reading/Language Arts Standards** for your grade. Throughout the book, special symbols (such as ) and codes (such as **R 1.1.2**) have been added to show where and how these standards are met. They will help you know *what* you are learning and *why*.

What do these symbols mean?

(CA) = Tested Standards in California

 = Skill or Strategy that will appear on your test

R = Reading Standards

W = Writing Standards

LC = Language Conventions Standards

LAS = Listening and Speaking Standards

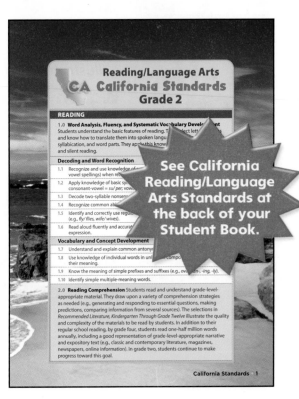

See California Reading/Language Arts Standards at the back of your Student Book.

Macmillan/McGraw-Hill

Unit 4

Teamwork

Better Together

Unit 5

Science

Growing and Changing

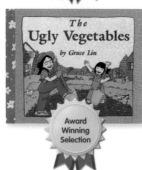

Unit 6

Spotlight on Grade 2
The World Around Us

THE BIG QUESTION

THEME: Plant and Animal Habitats

THEME: Animal Needs

Unit 4
Better Together

The Big Question

How is working together better than working alone?

Theme Launcher Video

 Find out more about teamwork at **www.macmillanmh.com**.

3

Some jobs are too big for one person to do. Jobs are easier and done faster when we work with other people. Cleaning up the classroom takes a short time when everyone helps. Construction workers work in teams to build bridges, buildings, and roads. To make communities safe at all times, some police officers work during the day, and others work at night. In this unit you will learn different ways people work together to complete big tasks. Learning about teamwork will help you work together with other people to get big projects done quickly.

Research Activities

Throughout the unit you will gather information about different places where teamwork happens. Choose and then research one example of teamwork. Use your research to create a play with characters who work together to solve a problem.

Keep Track of Ideas

As you read, keep track of what you learn about teamwork in the Layered Book organizer. On the top flap, write "Better Together." On the second flap, write "Teamwork at home." On the third flap, write "Teamwork at school." On the fourth flap, write "Teamwork at play." On each layer, write facts you learn about each place where teamwork can happen.

FOLDABLES®
Study Organizer

Better Together

Teamwork at home

Teamwork at school

Teamwork at play

Research Toolkit

Conduct Your Unit 4 Research Online with:

Research Roadmap
Follow step-by-step guide to complete your research project.

Online Resources
- Topic Finder and other Research Tools
- Videos and Virtual Fieldtrips
- Photos and Drawings for Presentations
- Related Articles and Web Resources

California Web Site Links

 Go to **www.macmillanmh.com** for more information.

California People

William "Bill" Russell, Professional Basketball Player
After Bill Russell learned to play basketball in California, he changed the way people play the sport with his focus on teamwork and defensive skills.

CA **Talk About It**

Why is it helpful to work together to finish a project?

LOG ON Find out more about getting the job done at **www.macmillanmh.com**.

Getting the Job Done

✓ **Vocabulary**

gasped
attached
frantically
swung
delicious

✓ **Context Clues**

Context clues are words that help you figure out the meaning of a word.

When you breathe, you *take air into and out of your lungs.*

The Story of the Giant Carrot

by Rosa Manuel

One day Farmer Smith planted carrot seeds. The next morning he looked outside and **gasped**. He took a gulp of air because he was so surprised. A giant leaf was growing in the garden. He knew what would be **attached**. Giant leaves are joined to giant carrots!

Farmer Smith ran outside **frantically**. He was very, very excited. He jumped up and grabbed the leaf. It was so high, he **swung** from it! His body waved from side to side. Once his feet were back on the ground, he pulled on the leaf. The giant carrot would not come out.

First, he called to his family for help. The family pulled, but the carrot was too big. Then he asked his neighbors to help. They pulled so hard that they had to stop to catch their breath. Finally, he called to the dog and cow for help. They all pulled, and at last the carrot popped out!

The Smith family fed the whole town with the **delicious** carrot. Everyone said it was the best-tasting carrot they had ever eaten!

Reread for **Comprehension**

Reread

Cause and Effect
Rereading a story can help you understand the cause and effects of events in the story. A cause is why something happens. An effect is what happens. Use the chart as you reread the story to identify the effects of the giant carrot on the farmer.

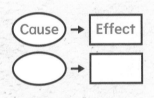

CA Comprehension

Genre
A **Folktale** is usually a made-up story that takes place long ago.

Reread
☑ **Cause and Effect**
As you read, use your Cause and Effect Chart.

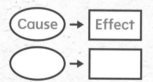

Read to Find Out
What causes the body parts to work together?

Head, Body, Legs

A Story From Liberia

Award Winning Author

retold by
Won-Ldy Paye & Margaret H. Lippert
illustrated by Julie Paschkis

Long ago, Head was all by himself.

He had no legs, no arms, no body. He rolled everywhere. All he could eat were things on the ground that he could reach with his tongue.

At night he rolled under a cherry tree. He fell asleep and dreamed of sweet cherries.

One morning Head
woke up and thought,
"I'm tired of grass and
mushrooms. I wish I could
reach those cherries."

He rolled himself up a
little hill. "Maybe if I get a
good head start I can hit the
trunk hard enough to knock some
cherries off," he thought. He shoved
with his ears and began to roll down
the hill. "Here I go!" he shouted.
Faster and faster he rolled.
CRASH!
"OWWWW!" he cried.

"Who's there?" someone asked.

Head looked up.
Above him **swung**
two Arms he had
never seen before.

"Look down here,"
Head said, "and
you'll see."

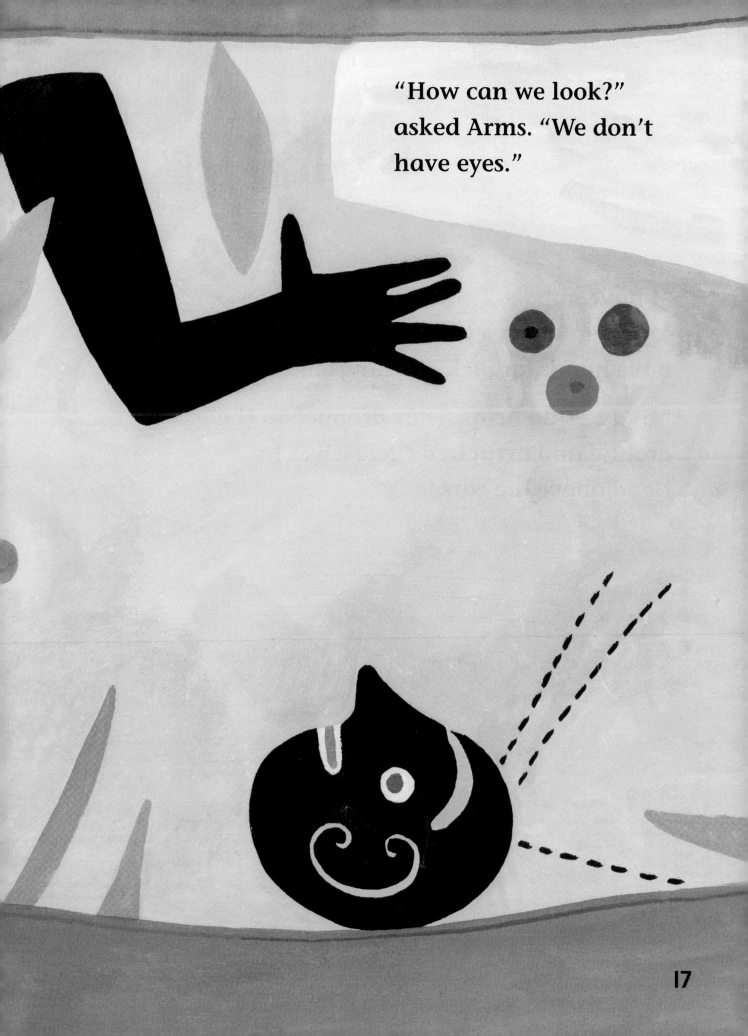

"How can we look?" asked Arms. "We don't have eyes."

17

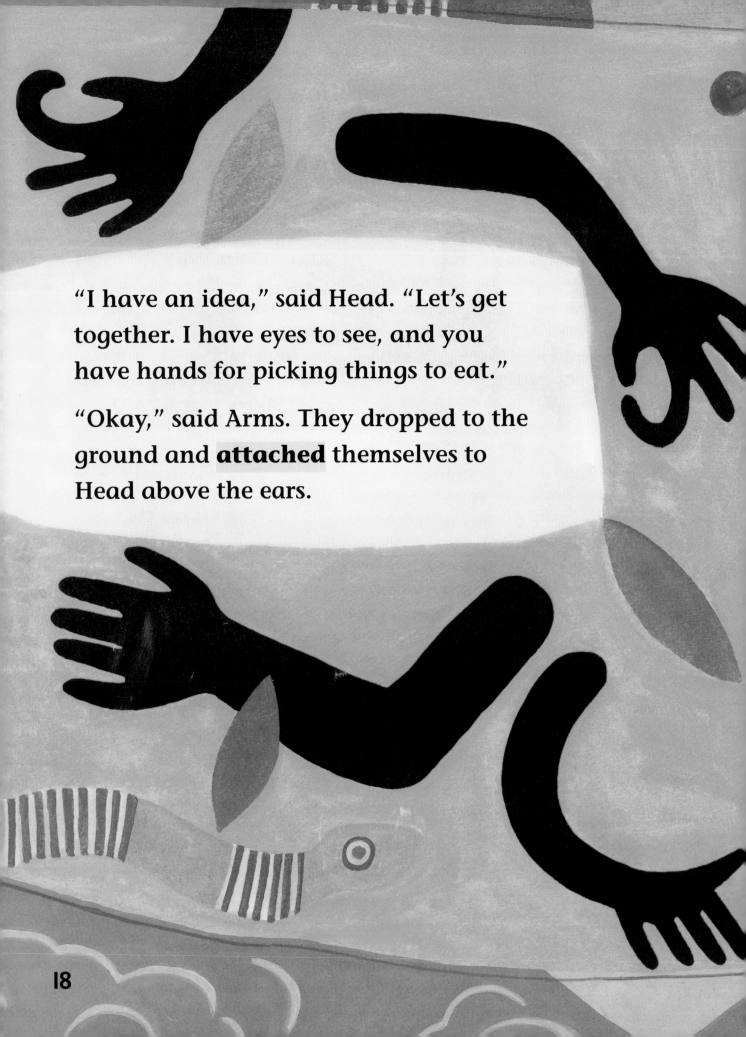

"I have an idea," said Head. "Let's get together. I have eyes to see, and you have hands for picking things to eat."

"Okay," said Arms. They dropped to the ground and **attached** themselves to Head above the ears.

"This," said Head, "is perfect."

Cause and Effect
Describe one possible effect of Arms and Head working together.

Hands picked cherries, and Head ate every single one.

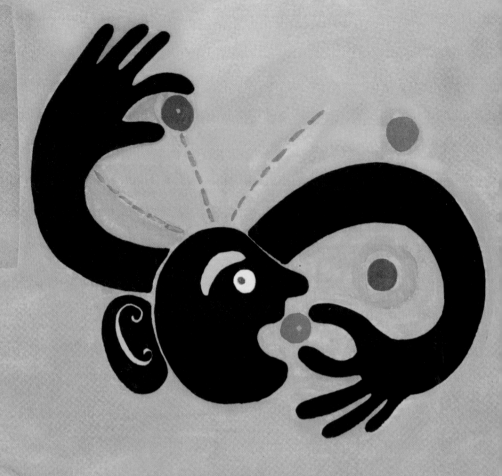

"It's time for a nap," said Head, yawning. Soon he was fast asleep.

While Head slept, Body bounced along and landed on top of him.

"Help!" **gasped** Head. "I can't breathe!" Arms pushed Body off.

"Hey," said Body. "Stop pushing me. Who are you?"
"It's us, Head and Arms," said Head. "You almost squashed us. Watch where you're going!"

"How can I?" asked Body. "I can't see."

"Why don't you join us?" said Head. "I see some ripe mangoes across the river. If you help us swim over there, I'll help you see where you're going."

"Okay," said Body. So Head attached himself to Body at the belly button.

"This," said Head,
"is perfect."

They bounced down the bank into the river.

"Pull right . . . pull left," Head shouted to Arms, who paddled **frantically** against the current.

Soon they reached the far bank and bounced up to the mango tree.

"Pick some," Head ordered. Arms stretched as high as they could, but they couldn't quite reach. Head looked around for a stick. Standing near the tree were two crossed Legs with feet on the ends.

"Get those," Head said to Arms.

Arms grabbed them.
"Let us go!" shouted Legs.

"Who are you?" asked Head.

"We're Legs. We were
walking but we bumped
into this tree."

"Join us," said Head. "I have eyes. I can show you where to go, and you can help us reach those mangoes."

"Okay," said Legs. So Legs attached themselves to the hands.

Cause and Effect
What causes Legs to join the other body parts?

"Not there," said Arms. "The hands need to be free to pick mangoes."

"I should be in the middle," said Body, "because I'm the biggest."

31

"That's right," said Head.
"You should be at the
bottom, Legs. I'll swing
around on top of Body so
I can see everything. And
Arms, you move to the
shoulders."

Everyone slid into place. Legs stood on tiptoe. Body straightened out. Arms stretched up and the hands picked a mango. Head took a bite.

"Mmm, **delicious**," Head said.
"Now THIS is perfect!"

Telling Stories with the Authors and Illustrator

Won-Ldy Paye came to this country from Liberia, which is in Africa. He is a storyteller as well as a writer. To write *Head, Body, Legs*, Won-Ldy worked with children's writer **Margaret Lippert**. Margaret travels all over the world learning folk stories. She shares her stories by writing children's books.

Artist **Julie Paschkis** is also a storyteller. She says she tells stories through her art. Julie has illustrated many children's books.

Another book by Won-Ldy Paye, Margaret Lippert, and Julia Paschkis

Mrs. Chicken AND THE Hungry Crocodile

Won-Ldy Paye & Margaret H. Lippert
Illustrated by Julie Paschkis

 LOG ON ▶ Find out more about Won-Ldy Paye and Julie Paschkis at **www.macmillanmh.com**.

CA **Author's Purpose**

Won-Ldy Paye and Margaret Lippert worked together to tell a story. Think about a time you worked with others to do something. What did you do? Write about the experience.

CA Critical Thinking

Retell the Story

Use the Retelling Cards to retell the story.

Retelling Cards

Think and Compare

1. What is the **effect** of all the body parts joining together? Use details from the story to explain how the parts help one another. **Reread: Cause and Effect**

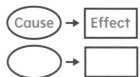

2. Reread pages 30–33. Why do the body parts change places several times? **Analyze**

3. What happened when Head and Arms **attached** themselves to each other? Do you think Head did the right thing? Explain. **Evaluate**

4. What did you learn from this tale? How is it important in real life? **Apply**

5. How is *Head, Body, Legs* like "The Story of the Giant Carrot" on pages 8–9? **Reading/Writing Across Texts**

CA Science

Genre
Nonfiction An Internet article gives facts about a topic and is found on the World Wide Web.

Text Feature
The Drop-Down Menu in an Internet article has links to related information on the Web site.

Content Vocabulary

force

friction

gravity

Watch It Move!

Rolling a ball and pulling a wagon are both examples of **force**. Force changes the way an object moves. Force can be a push, like when you roll a ball to a friend. Force can also be a pull, like when you drag a wagon.

Another force is called **friction**. Friction is when two things rub against each other. A ball slows down because of friction with the floor.

Gravity is a force, too. Hold a ball over your head and let it go. The ball will fall because Earth's **gravity** pulls it down.

Force and Motion Links

For more information about force and motion check out:

- Experiments in Force and Motion
- The Force of Gravity
- Understanding Friction

CA Critical Thinking

1. What other information about force can you link to in this article? **Drop-Down Menus**
2. Think about this article and *Head, Body, Legs: A Story from Liberia*. What kind of force do the arms use to paddle across the river? **Reading/Writing Across Texts**

Science Activity

Research force and motion activities online. Choose an activity and show it to the class.

 Find out more about force and motion at **www.macmillanmh.com**.

Writing

✓ A Strong Paragraph

A **strong paragraph** has a topic sentence and details that support it.

This is the topic sentence of my paragraph.

I include details that give more information about my topic.

Teamwork in the Park

Last month my whole class worked together to clean up the town playground. It was a big job. Pieces of paper and empty cans covered the ground. All 15 students worked as a team to throw away the garbage. It took more than four hours to get the job done. I am glad there were so many people to sweep and put trash in bags. Thanks to teamwork, the playground is now a clean and fun place for kids to play!

Your Writing Prompt

Some jobs are too big for one person to do alone.

Think about a time when you worked in a group to get something done.

Now write a personal narrative about that event.

Writer's Checklist

✓ My writing clearly tells about a time when I worked in a group.

✓ My writing is a **strong paragraph** with a topic sentence and supporting details.

☑ The details in my writing give more information about the topic.

✓ I put capital letters and punctuation in the right places. I use linking verbs correctly.

Describe ways people and animals can work together as a team.

LOG ON ▶ Find out more about special teams at www.macmillanmh.com.

Special Teams

SAFETY AT SCHOOL

Vocabulary

- attention
- buddy
- accident
- tip
- enormous
- obeys

Context Clues

Synonyms are words that have almost the same meaning.

Enormous and *huge* are synonyms.

SAFETY AT SCHOOL

by Brian Sullivan

"We need to talk about the school rules," our teacher, Mr. Wall, said. It was the second day of school. "What do you do when I turn out the lights?"

"Pay **attention** and listen carefully to you," said Pete.

"Good," said Mr. Wall. "What about lining up?"

"Find your line **buddy** and stand in line at the door," said Rosa.

"Right!" said Mr. Wall. "Remember, your line buddy is the friend you line up with. What is another rule, Julia?"

"No running in the halls," Julia said. "No one wants to fall or slip and have an **accident**."

"Good **tip**," said Mr. Wall. "That's helpful information to keep in mind. Also, why should we stay together in the halls?"

"This school is **enormous**. It's so huge it would be easy to get lost," said Liam.

"I know you all will follow the rules," said Mr. Wall. "When everyone **obeys** them, we stay safe."

Reread for **Comprehension**

Read Ahead
Use Illustrations
Reading ahead in a story can include looking at the illustrations. Looking at illustrations can help you understand the plot. Reread the story and use the chart to understand what the illustrations tell you about this story.

Illustration	What I Learn From the Picture

Comprehension

Genre
Fiction is a story with made-up characters and events.

Read Ahead

Use Illustrations
As you read and look at the pictures, use the Illustrations Chart.

Illustration	What I Learn From the Picture

Read to Find Out
How do the illustrations help make the story funny?

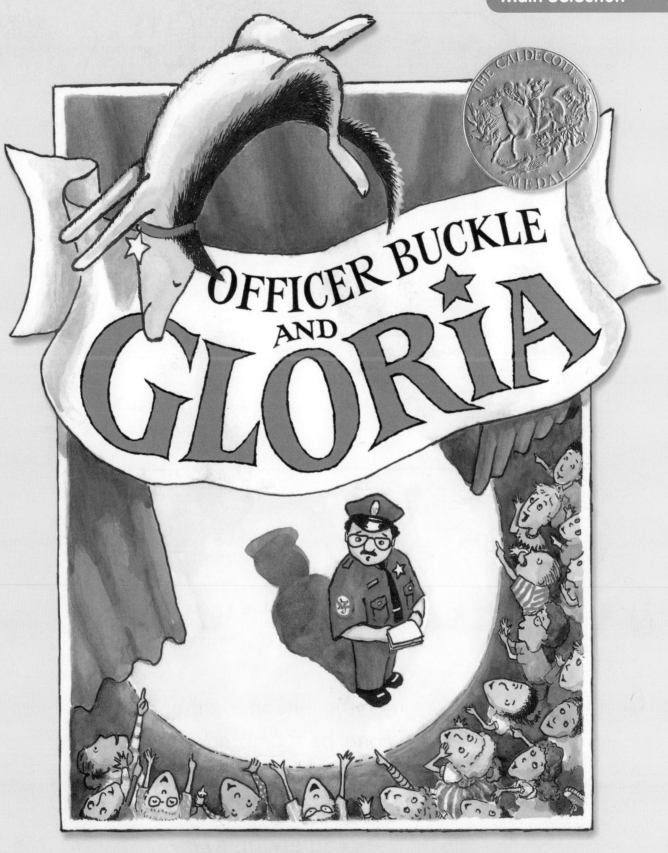

OFFICER BUCKLE AND GLORIA

**written and illustrated
by Peggy Rathmann**

47

Officer Buckle knew more safety **tips** than anyone else in Napville.

Every time he thought of a new one, he thumbtacked it to his bulletin board.

Safety Tip #77

NEVER stand on a SWIVEL CHAIR.

Officer Buckle shared his safety tips with the students at Napville School.

Nobody ever listened.

Sometimes, there was snoring.

Afterward, it was business as usual.

Mrs. Toppel, the principal, took down the welcome banner.

"NEVER stand on a SWIVEL CHAIR," said Officer Buckle, but Mrs. Toppel didn't hear him.

Then one day, Napville's police department bought a police dog named Gloria.

When it was time for Officer Buckle to give the safety speech at the school, Gloria went along.

"Children, this is Gloria," announced Officer Buckle. "Gloria **obeys** my commands. Gloria, SIT!" And Gloria sat.

Officer Buckle gave Safety Tip Number One:

"KEEP your SHOELACES tied!"

The children sat up and stared.
Officer Buckle checked to see if Gloria
was sitting at **attention**. She was.

"Safety Tip Number Two," said
Officer Buckle.

**"ALWAYS wipe up spills BEFORE
someone SLIPS AND FALLS!"**

The children's eyes popped.
Officer Buckle checked on
Gloria again.
"Good dog," he said.

Officer Buckle thought of a safety tip he had discovered that morning.

"NEVER leave a THUMBTACK where you might SIT on it!"

The audience roared.

Use Illustrations
Use the illustration to explain how Gloria makes Officer Buckle's speeches more interesting.

Officer Buckle grinned. He said the rest of the tips with *plenty* of expression.

The children clapped their hands and cheered. Some of them laughed until they cried.

Officer Buckle was surprised. He had never noticed how funny safety tips could be.

After *this* safety speech, there wasn't a single **accident**.

54

The next day, an **enormous** envelope
arrived at the police station. It was stuffed
with thank-you letters from the students at
Napville School.

Every letter had a drawing
of Gloria on it.

Officer Buckle thought
the drawings showed a lot
of imagination.

His favorite letter was written on a
star-shaped piece of paper. It said:

You and Gloria make a good team.

Your friend,
Claire

P.S. I always wear
a crash helmet.
(Safety Tip #7)

Officer Buckle was thumbtacking Claire's letter to his bulletin board when the phones started ringing. Grade schools, high schools, and day-care centers were calling about the safety speech.

"Officer Buckle," they said, "our students want to hear your safety tips! And please, bring along that police dog."

Officer Buckle told his safety tips to
313 schools. Everywhere he and Gloria went,
children sat up and listened.

After every speech, Officer Buckle took
Gloria out for ice cream.
   Officer Buckle loved having a **buddy**.

Then one day, a television news team videotaped
Officer Buckle in the state college auditorium.
When he finished Safety Tip Number Ninety-nine,

**DO NOT GO SWIMMING DURING
ELECTRICAL STORMS!,**

the students jumped to their feet and applauded.

"Bravo! Bravo!" they cheered.
Officer Buckle bowed again and again.

That night, Officer Buckle watched
himself on the 10 o'clock news.

Use Illustrations
What does Officer Buckle find out
about his safety speeches? Use the
illustrations to explain your answer.

63

The next day, the principal of Napville School telephoned the police station.

"Good morning, Officer Buckle! It's time for our safety speech!"

Officer Buckle frowned.

"I'm not giving any more speeches! Nobody looks at me, anyway!"

"Oh," said Mrs. Toppel. "Well! How about Gloria? Could she come?"

Someone else from the police station gave Gloria a ride to the school.

Gloria sat onstage looking lonely. Then she fell asleep. So did the audience.

After Gloria left, Napville School had its biggest accident ever....

It started with a puddle of banana pudding....

SPLAT!
SPLATTER!
SPLOOSH!

Everyone slid smack into Mrs. Toppel,
who screamed and
let go of her hammer.

The next morning, a pile of letters arrived at the police station.

Every letter had a drawing of the accident.

Officer Buckle was shocked.

At the bottom of the pile was a note written on a paper star.

Officer Buckle smiled.

The note said:

Gloria missed you yesterday!
Your friend,
Claire

P.S. Don't worry, I was wearing my helmet!
(Safety Tip #7)

Gloria gave Officer Buckle a big kiss on the nose. Officer Buckle gave Gloria a nice pat on the back. Then, Officer Buckle thought of his best safety tip yet…

Safety Tip #101

"ALWAYS STICK WITH YOUR BUDDY!"

A GOOD LAUGH WITH PEGGY RATHMANN

Peggy Rathmann got the idea for *Officer Buckle and Gloria* from a videotape. The tape shows Peggy's mother talking. In the background, their dog licks the eggs that were set out for breakfast.

The next part of the tape, Peggy says, "shows the whole family at the breakfast table, complimenting my mother on the delicious eggs." Of course, no one knew what the dog had done! "The first time we watched that tape we were so shocked, we couldn't stop laughing," Peggy says.

Other books written by Peggy Rathmann

Find out more about Peggy Rathmann at **www.macmillanmh.com**.

CA Author's Purpose

Peggy Rathmann wrote this story to show what can happen in the background. Have you ever done something behind the scenes without anyone knowing it? What did you do?

Critical Thinking

Retell the Story
Use the Retelling Cards to retell the story.

Retelling Cards

Think and Compare

1. What do the **illustrations** tell about Gloria's personality? Give details and information from the story to support your answer. **Read Ahead: Use Illustrations**

Illustration	What I Learn From the Picture

2. Reread pages 51–53. Why does no one listen to Officer Buckle's safety **tips**? Use the text and the illustrations to explain. **Apply**

3. Would you like to have a dog like Gloria? Why or why not? **Evaluate**

4. Why is "Always stick with your buddy" an important tip? **Synthesize**

5. How are the safety tips in "Safety at School" on pages 44–45 different from Officer Buckle's tips? **Reading/Writing Across Texts**

Genre
Nonfiction gives information about real people, things, or events.

Text Features
Floor Plans are maps that show where all the rooms in a building are.

Content Vocabulary
hazards
route
calm

Fire Safety

Firefighters want everyone to be safe. They teach families how to avoid fire **hazards**, which are dangerous items or situations. You can help prevent fires by following fire safety rules. You can also stay safe by knowing what to do if a fire starts nearby.

How to Stay Safe from Fire

- Never play with matches or lighters.

- Do not touch lit candles.

- Do not cook unless an adult is with you.

- Be careful around irons, stoves, fireplaces, and grills.

- Never touch electric cords, plugs, or outlets.

Stop! Drop! Roll!

If your clothes catch fire, do these three things right away.

1

Stop! Running and walking can make fire worse.

2

Drop! Get down on the ground. Cover your face and eyes.

3

Roll! Roll over and over until the flames are out.

73

Make a Plan!

You and your family can learn how to stay safe if there is a fire in your home. Make a floor plan of your home. Mark the best ways to get out of the house. Make sure your plan has more than one **route** in case one path gets blocked. Pick a safe place to meet outside. Have fire drills to practice your plan. Practicing will help you stay **calm** and find a safe path to the outside.

Fire Safety Floor Plan

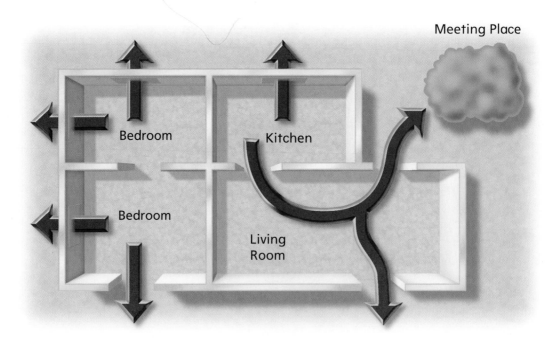

This floor plan shows several ways to get out of a home in case a fire starts.

After you are safely out of the house, call 9-1-1 for help. Wait for the firefighters to arrive. Never go back into the house for anything!

 Critical Thinking

1. What two escape routes from each bedroom does the floor plan show? **Floor Plan**

2. Think about this article and *Officer Buckle and Gloria*. What are some other safety tips that firefighters might try to teach to students and families? **Reading/Writing Across Texts**

 History/Social Science Activity

Draw a floor plan of your home. Show at least two escape routes and your outside meeting place. Give a copy to your family.

LOG ON ▶ Find out more about fire safety at www.macmillanmh.com.

Reading and Writing Connection

✓ **A Strong Opening**

Good writers create **strong openings** that interest their readers.

Wear Your Bike Helmet

by Jay F.

I wrote a strong opening sentence that tells about my essay topic.

My opening has a description.

I love riding my bike really fast, but I have learned how to be safe. Wearing a bike helmet every time you ride is important. Just last week I fell off my bike. But when my head hit the street, my helmet protected it. What would have happened if I hadn't worn my helmet? I hate to think about it! My helmet keeps me from getting really hurt. So be safe! Wear your bike helmet each time you ride!

76

Your Writing Prompt

Safety is very important.

Think about something you do
that helps you stay safe.

Write an essay about how people
can stay safe.

 Writer's Checklist

✓ My essay is clearly about something people
can do to stay safe.

☑ I include a **strong opening** to interest
readers.

✓ I include important details that illustrate
why safety is important.

✓ I use helping verbs correctly. All my
sentences end with a punctuation mark.

Describe some jobs that require groups of adults to work together.

 Find out more about worker teams at www.macmillanmh.com.

Worker Teams

Paramedics come when someone is sick or hurt.

A Ride to Help

The lights flash and the sirens scream. An ambulance is on its way. There is a **serious** problem. Someone is hurt or very sick.

Paramedics drive the ambulance. They also give help to people on the way to the hospital. Inside the ambulance are medical supplies. If someone has a broken bone, the paramedics use special tools to keep it still.

Paramedics take a **personal** interest in helping people. They give **aid** and get people to the hospital as quickly as possible.

Time for an X Ray

Who needs an X ray? People who have broken a bone will usually get an X ray taken at the hospital. An X ray is a special kind of photograph that shows bones and other parts inside the body.

What happens when you get an X ray? First, an X-ray worker takes the picture. Then, a doctor looks at the X ray to find out if a bone is broken. Last, the doctor **informs** the patient about how the bone will **heal**. She may tell the patient that he or she needs a cast. The doctor also explains that the bone will mend over time.

LOG ON ▶ Visit a hospital at **www.macmillanmh.com**.

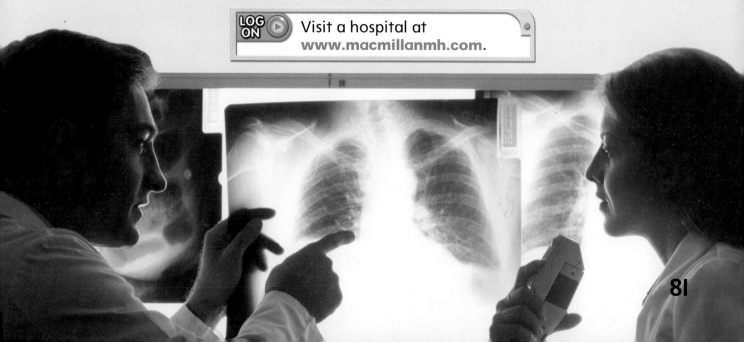

A Trip to the Emergency Room

Who works in the emergency room?

CA Comprehension

Genre
Nonfiction gives information about real people, things, or events.

Text Structure
✓ Sequence of Events
Sequence is the order in which things happen.

Oh, no! You have a broken bone. Where do you go? To the hospital emergency room, of course. The emergency room can be a busy place. Ambulances and people arrive there during the day and night. People are brought there if they have a **serious** medical problem.

Doctors and nurses work in the emergency room. Their job is to **aid** people who are sick or hurt. Other people help patients, too. They help keep the hospital running properly. Let's meet some of the people who work in a hospital emergency room.

82

H **Admissions Worker**

The first person you see in the emergency room is an admissions worker. The hospital needs to keep track of the patients coming into the emergency room. The admissions person checks you in. The adult who is with you will fill out hospital forms. The forms ask for your **personal** information and why you came to the hospital.

Next, a nurse will help you. A nurse's job is to find out about your injury and ask you questions about your health. The nurse will take your temperature and blood pressure and record this information on a chart. The nurse **informs** other people in the hospital about your problem.

Then you will meet an orderly, or nurse's aide. That person will help you get around in the hospital. She will take you to the correct department if you need to get tests done. She may use a wheelchair to take you from one area to another.

84

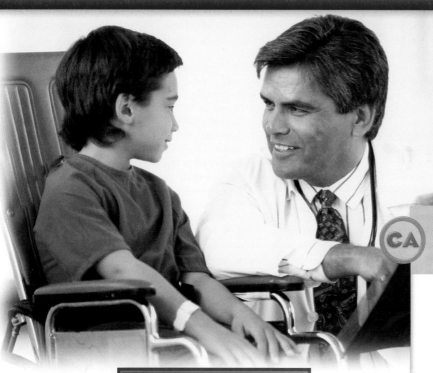

Doctor

Last, it's time for the doctor to examine you. The doctor checks your injury. He also looks at your chart. He arranges for you to get an X ray if you need one. The doctor knows how to fix your broken bone. He will probably put on a cast so the bone will **heal**. The doctor also decides whether you need to stay in the hospital or if you can go home right away.

So don't worry if you need to go to the emergency room. Now you know about the people who work there and how they will help you feel better.

CA Critical Thinking

1. Name the people you see in the hospital emergency room in the order you meet them. Use the words *first*, *next*, and *last*.

2. Why does the hospital need an admissions worker?

3. Have you ever gone to the hospital or the emergency room? If yes, tell about it. If no, tell about a time you went to the doctor.

4. How are paramedics similar to doctors? How are they different?

Show What You Know

Author and Me
The answer is not there on the page. Connect the clues to figure it out.

A Visit to the Dentist

You need your teeth to eat. To take good care of them, eat healthful foods, and remember to brush and floss every day. It's also important to visit the dentist every six months.

Here's what happens at a dental checkup. First, the dentist takes X rays. These pictures of your teeth show if you have any cavities. They also show the health of your teeth and gums. Next, the dentist or an assistant cleans your teeth and makes them shine.

Last, the dentist looks carefully inside your mouth. He or she uses a little mirror to see the teeth in the back of your mouth. The dentist is pleased when your teeth and gums are healthy! In six months it will be time to come back for another checkup.

Go on ▶

Now answer Numbers 1 through 4. Base your answers on the article "A Visit to the Dentist."

1. **What can a dentist teach you?**

   A how to read X rays

   B how to become a dentist

   C a new way to eat your food

   D the right way to brush your teeth

2. **Why do dentists look inside your mouth?**

   A to see if you eat healthful foods

   B to check the X rays

   C to look for problems

   D to use a little mirror

   Tip
   Connect the clues.

3. **Why is it important to get regular checkups?**

   A to get new dental floss

   B to make sure your gums are shiny

   C to check for tooth and gum problems before they get serious

   D to meet the new dental assistants

4. **What might a dentist tell you about taking care of your teeth? Use information from the article to support your answer.**

Write on Demand

Pat wrote a personal narrative about a librarian who helped him.

I put the events in order to organize my writing.

Help at the Library

I went to the library last summer. There were so many books! I asked the librarian for help.

First, Ms. Valdez asked me what I liked to read. I said I liked both made-up stories and true stories. Next, Ms. Valdez helped me find two good books. One was fiction, about a talking cat. The other book was nonfiction. It was about a paramedic.

Last, I took the books home. They were both fun to read. Now I always ask Ms. Valdez for help at the library. She really knows how to find the right books for me.

Your Writing Prompt

Respond in writing to the prompt below. Write for 8 minutes. Write as much as you can, as well as you can. Review the hints below before and after you write.

There are many people who can help you.

Think of a time when a worker helped you.

Write about how and why this person helped.

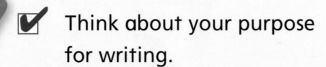

Writing Hints for Prompts

- ✔ Think about your purpose for writing.

- ✔ Plan your writing before beginning.

- ✔ Make sure the events in your writing are told in a clear sequence.

- ✔ Use your best spelling, grammar, and punctuation.

Community Teams

CA **Talk About It**

How do different people in your town work together to accomplish a goal?

LOG ON ▶ Find out more about community teams at www.macmillanmh.com.

91

A WHALE IS SAVED!

by Elizabeth Baker

A **young** whale got stuck in Drew Harbor today. The whale was small and had been born recently. Some people saw the whale in trouble. They called the police.

Soon help was on the way. Jenny Litz arrived first. She is a scientist who **examines** whales.

92

Jenny looks at every part of an animal to see if it is healthy. A whale is a **mammal**. Mammals are warm-blooded animals that have hair and drink their mother's milk. Jenny checked the whale's heartbeat and breathing. She said the whale seemed **normal**. There were no signs of illness.

Next, Jenny checked to see if **hunger** was a problem. Going a long time without food can be dangerous for a whale. But this whale seemed healthy and well fed.

The helpers acted fast. They kept the animal wet. The tide slowly came in. The water got deeper. Soon the whale could swim again. At last, the whale was **rescued**! Jenny and the other helpers saved the whale's life.

Reread for Comprehension

Summarize

Sequence of Events
One way to summarize an article is to describe the sequence of events. Reread the article and use the chart to help you understand what happens first, next, and last to save the whale.

First
Next
Last

CA Comprehension

Genre
Nonfiction is a retelling of a true event.

Summarize
Sequence of Events
As you read, use your Sequence Chart.

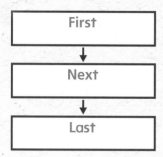

First

↓

Next

↓

Last

Read to Find Out
How is Sidney found, helped, and released to her ocean home?

94

A Harbor Seal Pup Grows Up

by Joan Hewett

photographs by Richard Hewett

By the Ocean

The harbor seal pup is 2 weeks old.
Her name is Sidney. Sidney stays close to
her mother. She drinks her mother's milk.

Waves crash on the rocky beach. Harbor
seal families lie in the warm sun.

Sidney and her mother lie in the sun too.

Sidney's mother gets hungry. She dives in the water to catch fish. The water is too cold for Sidney. So Sidney stays on the shore.

The seal pup waits for her mother. She waits for 3 days. She is very hungry.

People notice the seal pup. She is alone. Will her mother come back?

The next day, the pup is still alone. The people call for help. Sidney is **rescued**.

Sequence of Events
Think about the sequence of events. Describe how Sidney ends up alone on the beach.

Nursed Back to Health

Sidney is brought to a sea **mammal** center.

A scientist named Peter is in charge. Peter takes care of **young** seals. He lifts the thin pup from her cage.

Sidney is weak from **hunger**. Peter knows just what to do. He puts a tube in Sidney's mouth.

Then Nicole pumps a drink into Sidney's stomach. The drink is like a mother seal's milk.

Sidney is full. She is also very tired.
She falls asleep.

When Sidney wakes up, her eyes are
bright. She looks around.

Peter **examines** the pup. Her heartbeat is **normal**. So is her temperature. She is healthy.

Sidney has a full set of teeth. That means she is at least 3 weeks old. Sidney is small for her age.

Sidney gets her drink 3 times a day. She becomes stronger. Using her flippers, she scoots around.

A child's plastic pool becomes Sidney's playpen. She likes the water. She swims faster and faster.

Nicole shows Sidney a fish. Sidney does
not want it.

Nicole does not give up. Day after day,
she wiggles a fish in front of Sidney.
Then one day, the pup swallows it.

Before long, Sidney wants to eat fish. She waits for her bucket of fish in the morning.

The pup is gaining weight. She no longer needs her healthy drink.

Sidney is 5 weeks old. She has a thick layer of fat. The fat will keep her warm in cold water.

Sidney is ready to be on her own.

Sequence of Events
Describe the sequence of events that people take to help Sidney at the sea mammal center.

Returning to the Ocean

Peter puts the pup in a carrying case. Other scientists take over. They carry Sidney onto a boat. Sidney is excited by the ocean's salty smell. She shakes the case.

The boat heads toward an island. When they are almost there, the boat stops. It is time to say good-bye.

A scientist tips the case. "Good luck, little one," she says.

Sidney slips into the water. She will find other seals. She will catch fish. Sidney will grow up in her ocean home.

Joan and Richard Hewett's Animal Adventures

Joan Hewett and her husband, **Richard Hewett**, created their first children's book in 1977. After that, Richard says, "I knew that this was what I wanted to do. Children's books are the best."

Joan and Richard have worked on more than 20 children's books together. Many of these books are about animals. Joan says, "We always enjoy doing books that bring us in close contact with animals. Still, photographing harbor seals and other wild animals takes patience. It's a challenge, and that's part of the fun."

Other books by Joan Hewett and Richard Hewett

Find out more about Joan Hewett and Richard Hewett at **www.macmillanmh.com**.

A GIRAFFE CALF GROWS UP
by Joan Hewett · photographs by Richard Hewett

A KOALA JOEY GROWS UP
by Joan Hewett · photographs by Richard Hewett

CA Author's Purpose

The Hewetts like to write about animals. Think about when you helped an animal or a person. Write a paragraph about how you helped.

 Critical Thinking

Retell the Selection

Use the Retelling Cards to retell the selection.

Retelling Cards

Think and Compare

1. What happened to Sidney at the beginning, the middle, and the end of the selection? Use details to describe the **sequence of events**. **Summarize: Sequence of Events**

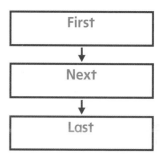

First
↓
Next
↓
Last

2. Reread pages 98–100. Sidney was very thin when she was **rescued**. Use the text to explain why. **Analyze**

3. How do you think the scientists felt saying good-bye to Sidney? Explain. **Evaluate**

4. Why do you think the scientists brought Sidney back to the ocean after she got healthy? **Analyze**

5. How is Sidney like the whale in "A Whale Is Saved" on pages 92–93? **Reading/Writing Across Texts**

Poetry

Genre
Poems can describe things in interesting or unusual ways.

✔ **Literary Element**
Similes compare one thing to another. A simile uses the words *like* or *as*. Similes help readers picture what something looks, sounds, or feels like.

The Puppy

Anonymous

Call the puppy,
And give him some milk.
Brush his coat
Till it shines like silk.
Call the dog
And give him a bone.
Go for a walk,
Then take him home.

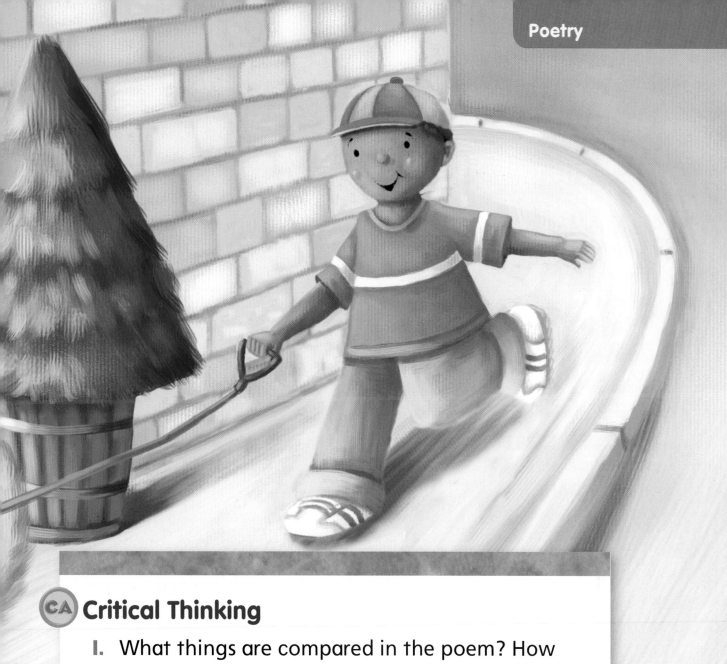

Critical Thinking

1. What things are compared in the poem? How can you tell that the comparison is a simile? **Simile**

2. Think about how the scientists cared for Sidney in *A Harbor Seal Pup Grows Up*. How is caring for a seal pup like caring for a puppy or a dog? How is it different? **Reading/Writing Across Texts**

LOG ON ▶ Find out more about animal care at **www.macmillanmh.com.**

Reading and Writing Connection

CA **Writing**

Important Details

Good writers use **important details** to make information in their writing clear to readers.

I give important details about the water.

This detail tells how often to brush Fred.

March 2, 2---

Dear Talia,

Thank you for taking care of my cat Fred while I am away. Taking care of Fred is easy! Starting tomorrow, give Fred two small cans of food each day. We already gave him food today. Fred needs a bowl of fresh water each morning, too. Please brush Fred's fur every two days. Fred needs lots of love so give him plenty of hugs.

Thanks for your help.

Sincerely,

Kim

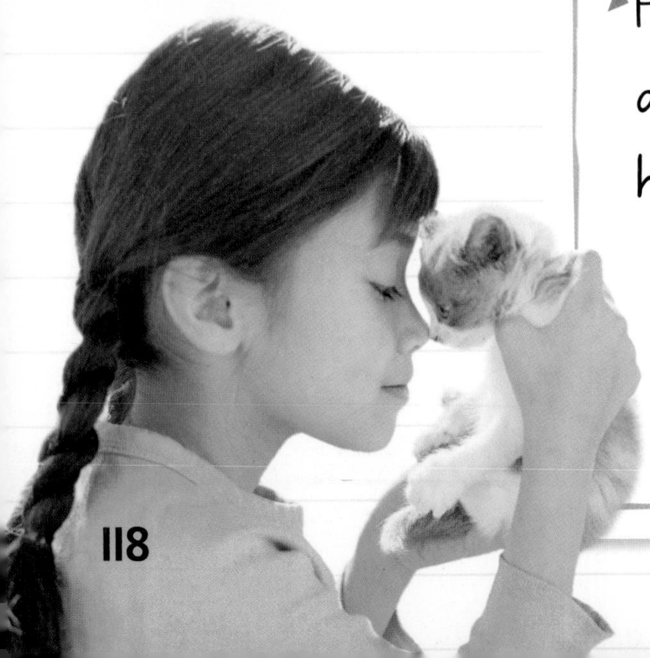

Your Writing Prompt

An animal you take care of could be your pet or the pet of someone you know.

Think about what to do to care for this animal.

Write a letter to a friend that tells how to take care of this pet.

Writer's Checklist

✓ My writing is about how to care for an animal.

✓ My letter is organized to describe events in the correct order.

☑ I include important details that make the information in my letter clear to readers.

✓ I use a capital letter to begin each sentence. I use irregular verbs correctly.

Surprising Teamwork

CA **Talk About It**

When have you
seen people
work together
in a surprising or
unusual way?

LOG ON ▶ Find out more about
surprising teamwork at
www.macmillanmh.com.

Bobo's celebration

by Keith Fish

Mom and I planned a surprise party for my brother Bobo.

First, my mom and I made a **menu**. It listed all the foods we would serve. The main dish was Bobo's favorite—seaweed stew!

Mom asked me to **fetch** the things we needed, so I swam to the Ship Shop. When I went to pay, I knew that I was forgetting something. I checked my list. I had not remembered the seaweed! So, I asked Ron Ray if he had any.

"Yes, I have some seaweed," he said. "That's 20 sand dollars, please." I paid him and swam home.

The day of the party, the stew **simmered** on the stove. I watched it bubble over low heat for hours.

An hour before the party, the guests **assembled** in one spot. The group gathered with Mom and me by the reef. When Bobo came, we yelled "Surprise!"

Bobo's party was fun. We **devoured** all of the stew. We ate until there was nothing left. Bobo said it was the best surprise ever!

Reread for **Comprehension**

Story Structure

Fantasy and Reality

A fantasy story could not happen in real life. A reality story could happen. Reread the story and use the chart to figure out whether "Bobo's Celebration" is a fantasy or reality story.

Reality	Fantasy
What Could Happen?	What Could Not Happen?

123

CA Comprehension

Genre
Fantasy has made-up characters, settings, or events that could not happen in real life.

Story Structure
✔ **Fantasy and Reality**
As you read, use your Fantasy and Reality Chart.

Reality	Fantasy
What Could Happen?	What Could Not Happen?

Read to Find Out
What do the mice do in this story that they can't do in real life?

Mice and Beans

by Pam Muñoz Ryan

illustrated by
Joe Cepeda

Award
Winning
Author

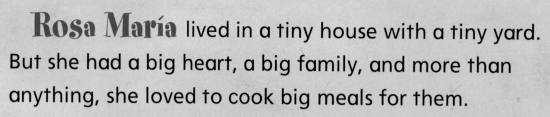

Rosa María lived in a tiny house with a tiny yard. But she had a big heart, a big family, and more than anything, she loved to cook big meals for them.

In one week, her youngest grandchild, Little Catalina, would be seven years old, and the whole family would squeeze into her *casita* for the party.

Rosa María didn't mind because she believed what her mother had always said: "When there's room in the heart, there's room in the house, **except** for a mouse."

Sunday, Rosa María planned the **menu**: *enchiladas*, rice and beans (no dinner was complete without rice and beans!), birthday cake, lemonade, and a *piñata* filled with candy.

She ordered the birthday present—something Little Catalina had wanted for a long time.

Satisfied with the plans, she wiped down the table so she wouldn't get mice and took out a mousetrap just in case. She was sure she had set one the night before, but now she couldn't find it. Maybe she'd forgotten.

When it was set and ready to **snap,** she turned off the light and went to bed.

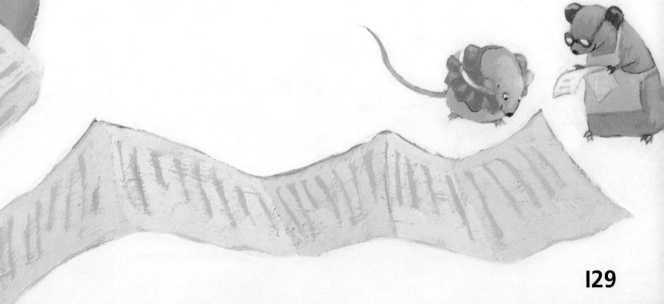

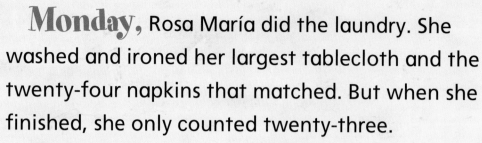

Monday, Rosa María did the laundry. She washed and ironed her largest tablecloth and the twenty-four napkins that matched. But when she finished, she only counted twenty-three.

"*No importa,*" she said. "It doesn't matter. So what if someone has a napkin that doesn't match? The important thing is that we're all together."

After dinner she swept the floor and checked the mousetrap.

But it was missing.

Didn't I set one last night? she wondered.

She hurried to the cupboard to **fetch** another, and when it was set and ready to **snap,** she turned off the light and went to bed.

130

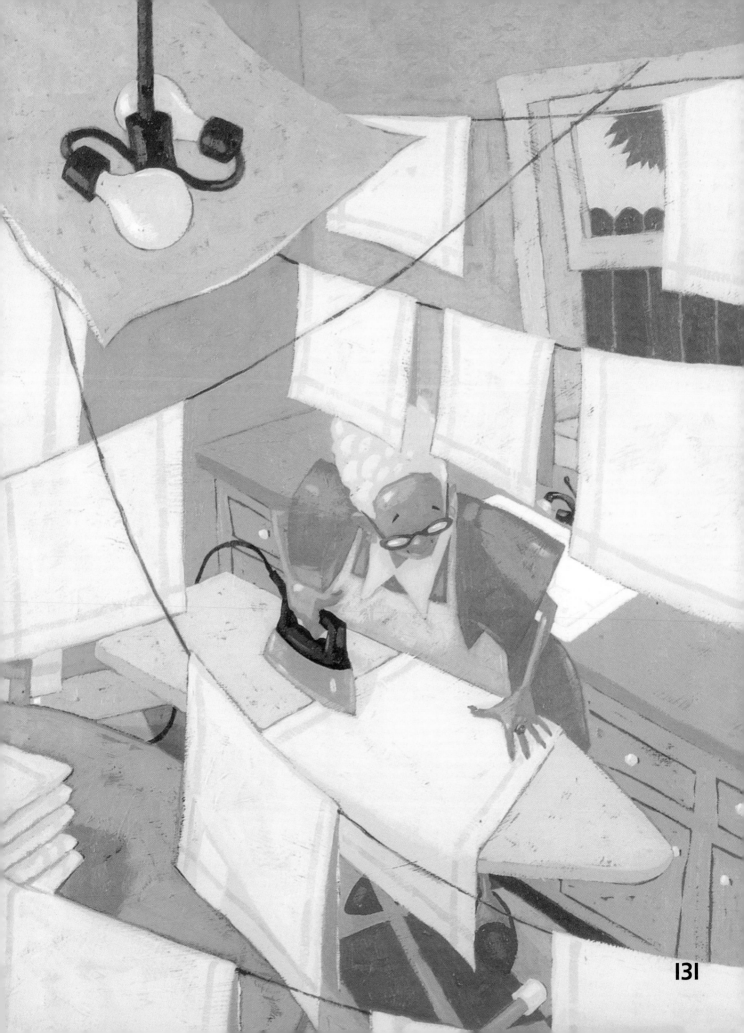

Tuesday, Rosa María walked to the market. She filled her big *bolsa* with *tortillas*, cheese, red sauce, white rice, pinto beans, and a bag of candy. She bought a *piñata* and on her way home she stopped at the *pastelería* to order the cake.

After dinner, she washed the dishes and checked the mousetrap.

But it had vanished.

"*¡Qué boba soy!* Silly me, I must have forgotten, again!"

She hurried to the cupboard to fetch another and when it was set and ready to **snap,** she turned off the light and went to bed.

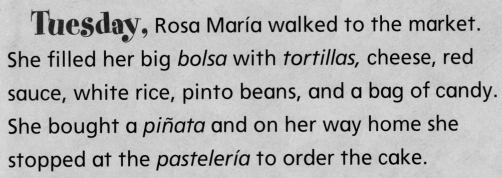

Fantasy and Reality
What clues do the illustrations give you that this story is a fantasy?

133

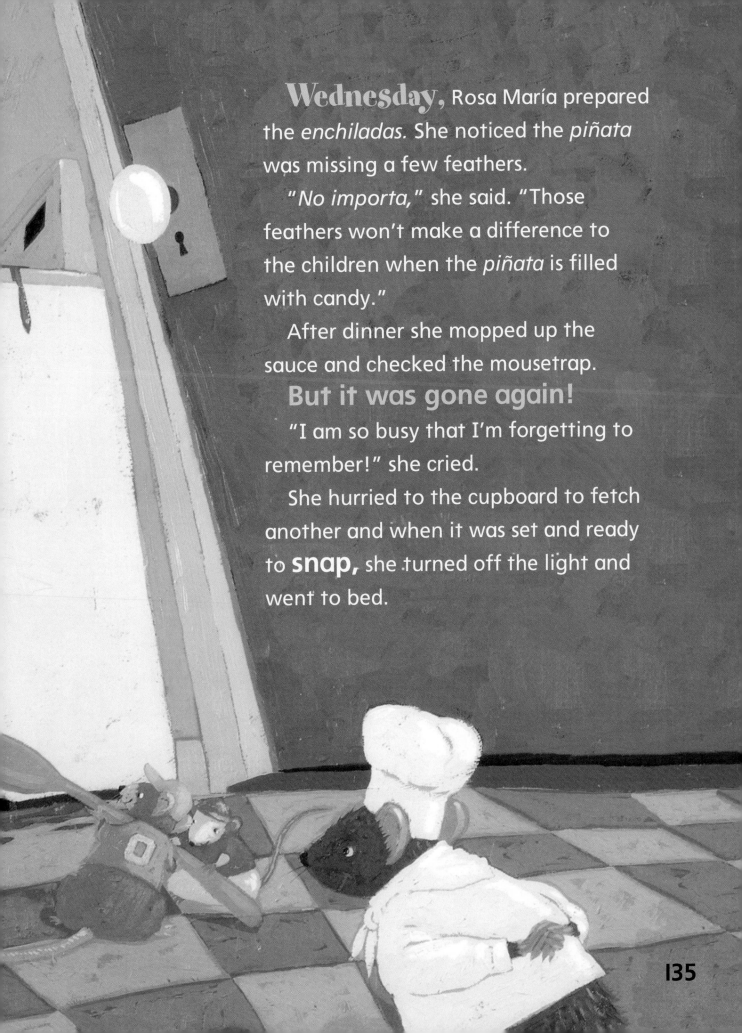

Wednesday, Rosa María prepared the *enchiladas*. She noticed the *piñata* was missing a few feathers.

"*No importa,*" she said. "Those feathers won't make a difference to the children when the *piñata* is filled with candy."

After dinner she mopped up the sauce and checked the mousetrap. **But it was gone again!**

"I am so busy that I'm forgetting to remember!" she cried.

She hurried to the cupboard to fetch another and when it was set and ready to **snap,** she turned off the light and went to bed.

Thursday, Rosa María simmered the beans. She searched for her favorite wooden spoon, the one she always used to cook *frijoles,* but she couldn't find it.

"*No importa,*" she said. "The beans will taste just as good if I use another spoon."

She added water all day long until the beans were plump and soft. Then she scrubbed the stove and checked the mousetrap.

But it was nowhere in sight!

"*¡Cielos!*" she said. "Heavens! Where is my mind?"

She hurried to the cupboard to fetch another and when it was set and ready to **snap,** she turned off the light and went to bed.

Friday, Rosa María picked up the cake and seven candles.

Tomorrow was the big day. Rosa María knew she mustn't forget anything, so she carefully went over the list one last time.

After dinner she wrapped the cake and checked the mousetrap.

She couldn't believe her eyes.

No mousetrap!

"Thank goodness I've got plenty."

She hurried to the cupboard to fetch another and when it was set and ready to **snap,** she turned off the light and went to bed.

Saturday, Rosa María cooked the rice. As the workers **assembled** Little Catalina's present, she set the table and squeezed the juiciest lemons from her tree.

"Let's see," she said, feeling very proud. "*Enchiladas,* rice and beans (no dinner was complete without rice and beans!), birthday cake, and lemonade. I know I have forgotten something, but what? **The candles!**"

But she only counted six.

"*No importa,*" she said. "I will arrange the six candles in the shape of a seven and Little Catalina will be just as happy. **Now,** everything is ready."

But WAS everything ready?

Fantasy and Reality
Describe two clues from the story that tell you if this is a fantasy or a realistic story.

143

That afternoon Rosa María's family filled her tiny *casita*. They ate the *enchiladas* and rice and beans. They drank the fresh-squeezed lemonade. And they **devoured** the cake.

Little Catalina loved her present—a swing set! And after every cousin had a turn, they chanted, "*¡La piñata! ¡La piñata!*"

They ran to the walnut tree and threw a rope over a high branch.

Whack! Whack! Little Catalina swung the *piñata* stick.

"Wait!" cried Rosa María as she remembered what she'd forgotten. But it was too late.

Crack! The *piñata* separated, and the children scrambled to collect the candy.

How could that be? Rosa María puzzled.
I must have filled it without even realizing!
She laughed at her own forgetfulness
as she hugged her granddaughter and
said, *"Feliz cumpleaños,* my Little Catalina.
Happy birthday."

After everyone had gone, Rosa María tidied her kitchen and thought contentedly about the *fiesta.* She pictured the happy look on Little Catalina's face when the candy spilled from the *piñata.* But Rosa María still couldn't remember when she had filled it.

"*No importa,*" she said. "It was a wonderful day."

But as Rosa María swept out the cupboard, she discovered the telltale signs of mice!

"*¡Ratones!*" she cried. "Where are my mousetraps? I will set them all!"

She inched to the floor and when she did, something caught her eye.

She looked closer.

Maybe I **didn't** fill the *piñata,* she thought.

"Was it possible?" she asked, shaking her head. "Could I have had help?"

Rosa María looked at the leftovers. Too much for one person.

And what was it her mother had always said? "When there's room in the heart, there's room in the house . . . **even** for a mouse."

"*¡Fíjate!* Imagine that!" she said. "I remembered the words wrong all these years."

Besides, how many could there be? Two? Four?

"*No importa,*" she said. "It doesn't matter if a few helpful mice live here, too."

Then she turned off the light and went to bed . . .

. . . and never set another mousetrap again.

152

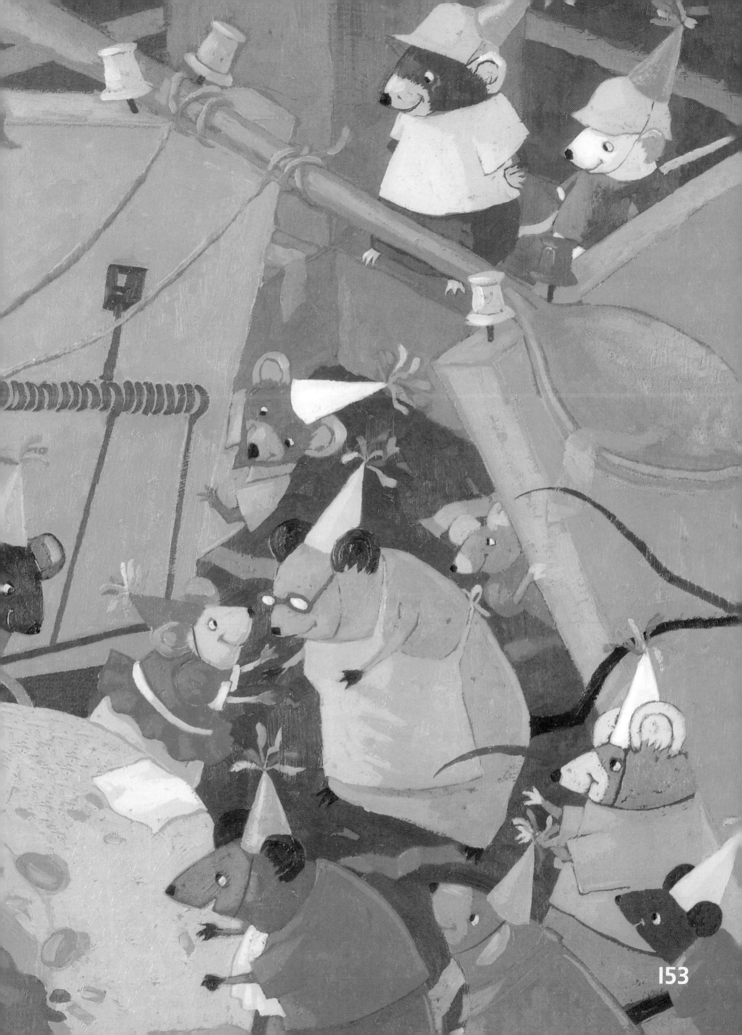

153

Celebrating with Joe Cepeda

Joe Cepeda says that many parties from his childhood looked just like the one in this book. For his son's parties, Joe always finds a special piñata. He has even made a hand-painted piñata stick. He hopes it will become a part of their family traditions.

Joe has received many awards for *Mice and Beans*. He has illustrated more than 15 other children's books. He also does artwork for magazines, newspapers, and businesses.

Other books illustrated by Joe Cepeda

LOG ON ▶ Find out more about Joe Cepeda at **www.macmillanmh.com**.

CA Author's Purpose
Joe Cepeda shares what he knows about parties. What traditions do you share in your family? What are some things your family does together? Write a paragraph about one of them.

Critical Thinking

Retell the Story
Use the Retelling Cards
to retell the story.

Retelling Cards

Think and Compare

1. Which parts of this
   story are **realistic**?
   Which could only
   happen in a **fantasy**?
   Use details from
   the story to support
   your answer. **Story
   Structure: Fantasy and Reality**

Reality	Fantasy
What Could Happen?	What Could Not Happen?

2. Reread pages 130–131. How do the illustrations
   help you understand why Rosa María must
   fetch another mousetrap? **Analyze**

3. What special foods or activities do you have at
   family gatherings? **Analyze**

4. Why do you think some people like to
   celebrate by having parties? **Evaluate**

5. How are "Bobo's Celebration," on
   pages 122–123, and *Mice and Beans* alike?
   What do both parties have in common?
   Reading/Writing Across Texts

Genre
Some **nonfiction** articles give you information about how to make a food or drink.

✓ **Text Feature**
Written Directions are steps that tell you how to make or do something.

Content Vocabulary
liquids
solids
gas

Rosa María's Rice and Beans

When you cook, you often mix **liquids** and **solids**, such as when you mix water and flour. These different states of matter can change in different ways as you cook them.

Heating some solids can make them turn brown. Other solids become soft when you heat them. Heating liquids can make them boil. If you boil liquid long enough, it can change its state. It becomes a **gas**, another state of matter.

In the following recipes you will mix solids and liquids to make Rosa María's rice and beans.

Rice

What You Need

2 tablespoons vegetable oil

⅓ cup minced onion

⅓ cup minced bell pepper

1 ½ cups long grain white rice

1 14 ½ -ounce can chicken or vegetable broth

¼ cup tomato sauce stirred into 1 ½ cups of water

What To Do

1. Pour the oil into a large skillet. Oil is a liquid.

2. Add the onion, bell pepper, and rice. These are solids. Sauté (SAW-tay), or fry, these solids over medium heat until rice is lightly toasted, and the vegetables are soft.

3. Add the liquids (broth and tomato sauce water) to the solids. Bring to a boil.

4. Cover, and turn the heat to low.

5. Simmer for 20 to 25 minutes, or until the liquid has been soaked up. Do not stir while simmering or the rice will be mushy.

Beans

What You Need

1 16-ounce bag dried pinto beans

1 large onion, chopped

4 cloves garlic, minced

2 14 ½ -ounce cans chicken or vegetable broth

2 14 ½ -ounce soup cans of water

   salt and pepper, add to taste

What To Do

1. Follow the directions on the back of the bag for cleaning and soaking the beans.

2. Drain the water (a liquid).

3. Combine the solids (beans, onions, and garlic) with the liquids (broth and water) in a large pot. Bring to a boil.

4. Cover pot. Reduce heat to low and simmer for 2 ½ to 3 hours. Stir often until beans are plump and soft.

Solid, Liquid, or Gas?

The same material can be in three different states—solid, liquid, and gas.

1. A solid has a definite size and shape. Ice is a solid. When water freezes, it becomes ice.

2. Liquid takes up space, but it does not have shape. Liquid in a container takes that container's shape. Water is a liquid.

3. Gas does not take up space or have shape. Steam is a gas. When water boils, it turns to steam.

CA Critical Thinking

1. What should you do to the beans while they are simmering? **Written Directions**

2. Think about the recipes and the story *Mice and Beans*. Rosa María planned a menu for the party. Write a menu that includes the food you would like to have at a party. **Reading/Writing Across Texts**

Science Activity

Think about your favorite recipe. Write about the solids, liquids, and gases in the recipe.

 LOG ON ▶ Find out more about different states of matter at www.macmillanmh.com.

Writing

CA

✔ Vary Words

Good writers **vary words** to make their writing clear, interesting, and more exact.

I use the word <u>annual</u> to tell how often field day happens.

I vary the words I use to describe the event.

Community Field Day!

The annual Washington Elementary School Field Day will take place on June 18.

Please join us for a day filled with exciting activities and terrific food. The fun starts at 1 p.m. at the school's football field.

This event is open to all students and their families. Take part in sack races, a water balloon toss, and an obstacle course! A picnic will follow the games. Don't miss this event!

Contact Ms. Cahill for more information.

Your Writing Prompt

A flyer or a poster can advertise or tell about an event.

Think about an event in your school or community.

Write an advertisement about this event.

Writer's Checklist

 My writing clearly advertises an event.

 I give information about what will happen at the event and where it will take place.

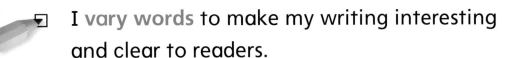 I **vary words** to make my writing interesting and clear to readers.

 I form contractions correctly. I capitalize and punctuate my sentences in the right places.

Chicken Little

One morning Chicken Little walked through the woods. **PLUNK!** An acorn fell on her head.

Chicken Little clucked, "The sky is falling! I must tell the queen!" She took the acorn with her to prove that the sky was falling.

She had not gone far when—**BUMP!**—she ran into Henny Penny.

Chicken Little clucked, "The sky is falling! We must tell the queen."

Chicken Little and Henny Penny ran. They had not gone far when—**THUMP!**—they bumped into Ducky Lucky.

Chicken Little and Henny Penny clucked, "The sky is falling! We must tell the queen."

Chicken Little, Henny Penny, and Ducky Lucky ran. They had not gone far when—**SCREECH!**—the three friends stopped. Standing before them was Foxy Loxy.

Sly Foxy Loxy smiled, showing his sharp teeth. "Good morning," he said. "What is your hurry?"

Chicken Little clucked, "The sky is falling. We must tell the queen."

Foxy Loxy's smile grew. "I will lead you to the queen," he said.

Chicken Little, Henny Penny, and Ducky Lucky followed Foxy Loxy. That crafty fox led them straight to his den. Before he could eat them, he heard the sounds of the queen coming near. Foxy Loxy was very afraid of the queen. He ran far, far away.

Chicken Little, Henny Penny, and Ducky Lucky told the queen about the sky falling. Chicken Little showed her the acorn.

"Silly animals," said the queen. "The sky is not falling. That acorn simply fell from a tree. Go home and do not worry about the sky anymore."

The three friends marched home and did exactly as the queen said.

163

Foolish, Timid Rabbit

Foolish, timid Rabbit sat under a coconut tree. He looked around the forest and said, "What will happen to me if the world falls apart?" **KERPLUNK!** A coconut crashed behind Rabbit.

Rabbit cried, "The world is falling apart!" He hopped away, yelling loudly.

Soon another rabbit saw him. "What are you yelling about?"

Rabbit cried, "The world is falling apart!" He hopped away, screaming even louder.

Soon the word spread from one rabbit to the next. In no time at all other forest animals heard the scary news. Deer told Buffalo. Buffalo told Rhinoceros. Rhinoceros told Elephant. Now all the animals were running and screaming.

Suddenly Lion stepped quietly from his cave. "Stop a moment, friends. Why are you running so fast?"

"The world is falling apart!" cried Rabbit. "I heard the first piece fall."

Lion nodded wisely. "Show me where it fell," he said.

Rabbit led Lion to the coconut tree.

Lion laughed when he saw the coconut on the ground. "Rabbit," he said. "You only heard a coconut fall. The world is safe and all in one piece. Do not bother the other animals with your nonsense."

"Foolish Rabbit," scolded the other animals. "If not for wise Lion, we would be running away forever."

CA Critical Thinking

Now answer questions 1 through 4.

Base your answers on the story "Chicken Little."

1. **Which words from the story are SYNONYMS?**
   A   ran, stopped
   B   walk, ran
   C   sly, crafty
   D   led, followed

2. **Chicken Little runs through the woods because**
   A   Foxy Loxy chases her.
   B   it is raining.
   C   the queen is waiting for her.
   D   she thinks the sky is falling.

3. **What happens FIRST in this story?**
   A   An acorn hits Ducky Lucky.
   B   An acorn hits Chicken Little.
   C   The animals meet the queen.
   D   The queen thinks the sky is falling.

4. **How can you tell that this story is a fantasy?**
   Use details from the story in your answer.

Now answer questions I through 4. Base your answers on the story "Foolish, Timid Rabbit."

1. **Which words from the story are SYNONYMS?**

   A screaming, yelling
   B foolish, wise
   C soon, suddenly
   D scolded, cried

2. **What happens LAST in this story?**

   A A coconut falls near Rabbit.
   B Deer tells Buffalo about the world falling apart.
   C The animals scold Rabbit.
   D Lion tells the animals they are safe.

3. **How does Rabbit feel when he tells the animals that the world is falling apart?**

   A angry
   B afraid
   C happy
   D calm

4. **What is the setting for this story?**

   A a big city
   B a river
   C a forest
   D a mountaintop

Write on Demand

PROMPT Compare and contrast the different versions of the same story from different cultures. How are "Chicken Little" and "Foolish, Timid Rabbit" alike? How are the stories different? Write for 8 minutes. Write as much as you can as well as you can.

The Big Question

How do animals and plants change as they grow?

Theme Launcher Video

LOG ON ▶ Find out more about how animals and plants change as they grow at www.macmillanmh.com.

169

Animals and plants go through specific changes during their lives. Some baby animals look a lot like their parents, such as kittens or bear cubs. Other animals change a lot as they grow up, such as a caterpillar changing into a butterfly. Plants change as they grow, too. Many plants start out as seeds. The seeds send roots into the ground and stems upward through the earth. These stems develop leaves and flowers, which contain new seeds for new plants.

Learning about animals and plants will help you care for them and better understand the natural world around you.

Research Activities

Throughout the unit you will gather information about plants and animals. Choose one animal or plant. Research that topic and then use your notes to create a Life Cycle Booklet for that plant or animal.

Keep Track of Ideas

As you read, keep track of all you are learning about animals and plants and how they change as they grow. Use the Two-Pocket Study Organizer. On the left pocket, write "Plants." On the right pocket, write "Animals." Each week record plant and animal facts on cards and put them in the appropriate pocket.

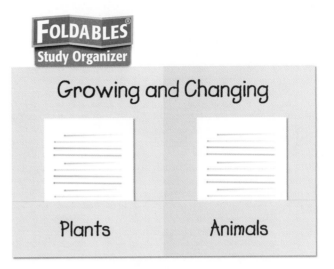

FOLDABLES®
Study Organizer

Growing and Changing

Plants   Animals

Research Toolkit

Conduct Your Unit 5 Research Online with:

Research Roadmap
Follow step-by-step guide to complete your research project.

Online Resources
- Topic Finder and other Research Tools
- Videos and Virtual Fieldtrips
- Photos and Drawings for Presentations
- Related Articles and Web Resources

California Web Site Links

 Go to **www.macmillanmh.com** for more information.

California People

Grafton Tyler Brown, Landscape Artist
Grafton Tyler Brown painted landscapes of plants and animals in the Pacific Northwest area in the 1800s.

CA **Talk About It**

How do plants change as they grow?

LOG ON ▶ Find out more about plants at www.macmillanmh.com.

A Plant's Life

Plant Power!

by Bradley Roberts

People use plants in many ways. All around us are objects that come from plants.

Your T-shirt probably started as a cotton plant. The cotton plant has seeds called bolls. Hot weather makes the bolls **burst**. When they break open, a soft fluff of cotton pops out. The fluff sometimes **drifts** in the air, moving slowly in the wind. People can spin the fluff into thread that becomes material.

Other plants are used to make medicines. Some of these plants are found in a dry, hot place like the **desert**. The aloe plant has a juice that helps heal cuts. Many people grow aloe plants. An aloe plant **drowns** easily. It is important not to give the plant too much water because it will die. To get the aloe juice, **gently** break off a leaf. Do it carefully to not harm the plant.

Some plants are so big that we can build with them. Many houses are made from trees. Look at the houses of the people who live near you. Does your **neighbor** have a wooden house?

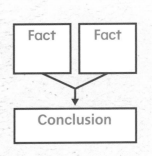

Reread for **Comprehension**

Summarize

Draw Conclusions

After you summarize this article, you can use the information in it and what you know from real life to draw conclusions. Reread the article and use the chart to draw conclusions about why plants are important to humans.

Fact | Fact

Conclusion

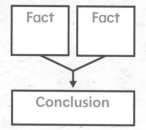
Genre
Fiction is a made-up story that may give information about a real-life topic.

Summarize
Draw Conclusions
As you read, use your Conclusions Chart.

```
┌───────┐   ┌───────┐
│ Fact  │   │ Fact  │
└───────┘   └───────┘
      │         │
      └────┬────┘
           ▼
   ┌────────────────┐
   │   Conclusion   │
   └────────────────┘
```

Read to Find Out
What does the tiny seed need to grow?

176

Award Winning Author

ERIC CARLE

The Tiny Seed

It is Autumn.
A strong wind is blowing. It blows flower seeds
high in the air and carries them far across
the land. One of the seeds is tiny,
smaller than any of the others.
Will it be able to keep up with the others?
And where are they all going?

One of the seeds flies higher than the others.
Up, up it goes! It flies too high and the sun's rays
burn it up. But the tiny seed sails on with the others.

Draw Conclusions
Use story details to draw
a conclusion about how
the wind helps the seed.

Another seed lands on a tall and icy mountain.
The ice never melts, and the seed cannot grow.
The rest of the seeds fly on. But the tiny seed
does not go as fast as the others.

Now they fly over the ocean.
One seed falls into the water and **drowns**.
The others sail on with the wind.
But the tiny seed does not go as high as
the others.

One seed **drifts** down onto the **desert**.
It is hot and dry, and the seed cannot grow.
Now the tiny seed is flying very low,
but the wind pushes it on with the others.

Finally the wind stops and the seeds fall **gently** down on the ground. A bird comes by and eats one seed. The tiny seed is not eaten. It is so small that the bird does not see it.

Now it is Winter.

After their long trip the seeds settle down.
They look just as if they are going to sleep
in the earth. Snow falls and covers them
like a soft white blanket. A hungry mouse
that also lives in the ground eats a seed
for his lunch. But the tiny seed lies very still
and the mouse does not see it.

Now it is Spring.

After a few months the snow has melted.
It is really Spring! Birds fly by. The sun shines.
Rain falls. The seeds grow so round and full
they start to **burst** open a little. Now they
are not seeds any more. They are plants.
First they send roots down into the earth.
Then their little stems and leaves begin to grow
up toward the sun and air. There is another plant
that grows much faster than the new little
plants. It is a big fat weed. And it takes all
the sunlight and the rain away from one of
the small new plants. And that little plant dies.

The tiny seed hasn't begun to grow yet.
It will be too late! Hurry!
But finally it too starts to grow into a plant.

The warm weather also brings the children out to play. They too have been waiting for the sun and spring time. One child doesn't see the plants as he runs along and—Oh! He breaks one! Now it cannot grow any more.

The tiny plant that grew from the tiny seed is growing fast, but its **neighbor** grows even faster. Before the tiny plant has three leaves the other plant has seven! And look! A bud! And now even a flower!

But what is happening? First there are footsteps.
Then a shadow looms over them. Then a hand
reaches down and breaks off the flower.
A boy has picked the flower to give to a friend.

It is Summer.

Now the tiny plant from the tiny seed
is all alone. It grows on and on. It doesn't stop.
The sun shines on it and the rain waters it.
It has many leaves. It grows taller and taller.
It is taller than the people. It is taller than
the trees. It is taller than the houses.
And now a flower grows on it. People come
from far and near to look at this flower.
It is the tallest flower they have ever seen.
It is a giant flower.

192

All summer long the birds and bees and butterflies come visiting. They have never seen such a big and beautiful flower.

Now it is Autumn again.

The days grow shorter. The nights grow cooler. And the wind carries yellow and red leaves past the flower. Some petals drop from the giant flower and they sail along with the bright leaves over the land and down to the ground.

Draw Conclusions
Think about the beginning of the story. Draw a conclusion about what may happen to the flower next.

197

The wind blows harder. The flower has lost almost all of its petals. It sways and bends away from the wind. But the wind grows stronger and shakes the flower. Once more the wind shakes the flower, and this time the flower's seed pod opens. Out come many tiny seeds that quickly sail far away on the wind.

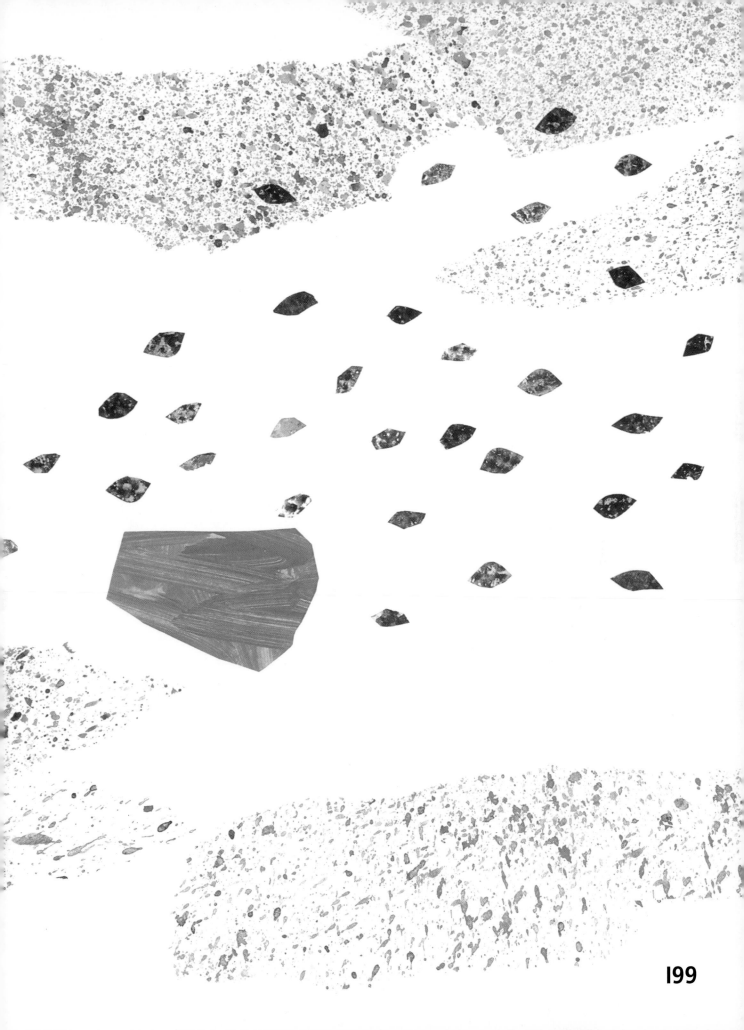

Cut, Paste, and Learn with Eric Carle

Eric Carle has illustrated more than 70 books. He wrote most of these books, too. Many books, such as *The Tiny Seed*, are about nature.

Eric's artwork is called *collage*. First, he paints on paper. Then he cuts it into small shapes. He glues the painted paper in layers to make the larger shapes he wants.

Eric says, "I want to show [children] that learning is really both fascinating and fun."

Other books written and illustrated by Eric Carle

Find out more about Eric Carle at **www.macmillanmh.com**.

CA Author's Purpose

Eric Carle explains what happens to a seed. Think about a flower, plant, or tree. Describe what the plant looks like and how it grows.

Critical Thinking

Retell the Story
Use the Retelling Cards to retell the story.

Retelling Cards

Think and Compare

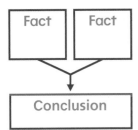

1. **Draw a conclusion** about how being very small helps the tiny seed. Use details from the story to support your answer. **Summarize: Draw Conclusions**

2. Reread page 192. How does being all alone in summer help the tiny plant? **Analyze**

3. What new information did you learn about plants and seeds from the story? What did you know already? **Evaluate**

4. Why does the story end with the flower making new seeds? What do you think will happen to the new seeds? **Synthesize**

5. "Plant Power!" on pages 174–175 tells about how cotton bolls **burst**. Based on what you learned in *The Tiny Seed*, how do you think cotton seeds are spread? **Reading/Writing Across Texts**

Plant Parts

by Pilar Jacob

A plant is a living thing. It uses its many parts to grow from a small **seed** to a large plant. Each part helps the plant stay healthy. Plants also need **sunlight** to grow. They get light from the sun and **minerals** from the soil. These things help the plant stay alive and grow.

Flowers
Flowers make seeds that can grow into new plants.

Stem
The stem helps hold up the plant. It moves the food and water from the roots to the other parts of the plant.

Leaves
Leaves use sunlight, water, and air to make food.

Roots
A plant grows roots under the ground. The roots hold the plant in place.

202

Fruit
Some plants have fruit. The fruit grows around the seeds and keeps them safe.

Seeds
Seeds can grow into new plants.

 Critical Thinking

1. What are two ways that roots help a plant stay alive? **Diagrams and Labels**

2. Look at the picture of the giant flower at the end of the *The Tiny Seed*. Draw a picture that looks like this flower. Label each of the plant parts. **Reading/Writing Across Texts**

 Science Activity

Research a plant that grows fruit. Make a diagram of this plant and label each part.

 Find out more about plants at www.macmillanmh.com.

203

Writing

✔ Important Details

Details can give readers important information on how to do something.

These details tell what I need to do this project.

These steps give details about how best to grow the flowers.

How to Grow Marigolds

You will need marigold *seeds*, a pot with *soil*, and *water*.

marigold *seeds*   pot with *soil*   *water*

1. Make two holes in the soil about two inches apart. Make each hole one inch deep.
2. Put two *seeds* in each hole. Cover them with soil.
3. Put the pot in a *sunny* place.
4. Water it about every four days. Watch your marigolds grow!

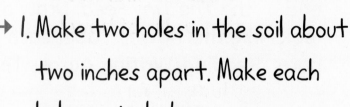

Your Writing Prompt

A poster can show how to do something.

Think about what you know how to do and would like to share.

Make a poster. Write the steps that tell what to do. Draw pictures with labels to show what is needed.

Writer's Checklist

☑ My writing is about how to do something.

☑ I include numbered steps that show the correct order of how to do something.

☐ I include important details that help the reader know exactly what to do.

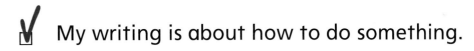

☑ My sentences are complete. I use the correct end punctuation. I use pronouns correctly.

Garden Plants

Talk About It

What do people grow in gardens? What is needed to grow a garden?

LOG ON ▶ Find out more about garden plants at www.macmillanmh.com.

207

City Garden

by Roberto Salazar

Vocabulary

- scent
- trade
- muscles
- prickly
- blooming
- aroma

Context Clues

Homophones are words that sound the same but have different spellings and different meanings.

Scent and *cent* are homophones.

Scent means smell. A *cent* is money.

When we lived in the country, Dad and I had a garden. We planted beans, peas, and other vegetables. To us, the **scent** of moist soil and growing plants was a kind of perfume. We loved the earthy smell.

Then we moved to the city. We had to **trade** our big country garden for a small city window box.

Dad and I missed the garden. So he offered to help my class plant a garden in an empty lot.

First, my class dug up the soil in the lot. We needed strong **muscles** to do all that hard work.

Next, we planted seeds and small plants in neat rows. We wore gloves because some plants had sharp, **prickly** thorns.

Soon the flowers were **blooming**. The lot reminded me of my old garden. It was great to smell the fresh **aroma** of plants that filled the air. Then, tiny vegetables grew. Last, the vegetables became large and ripe, so we picked them. Dad and I enjoyed some tasty vegetables from our city garden.

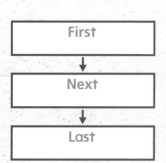

Reread for Comprehension

Summarize

Sequence of Events

You can summarize an article by retelling the sequence of events, or what happened first, next, and last. Reread the article and use the Sequence Chart to describe the sequence of events that the class takes to plant a garden.

First
↓
Next
↓
Last

CA Comprehension

Genre
Realistic Fiction is a made-up story that could happen in real life.

Summarize
✔ **Sequence of Events**
As you read the story, use the Sequence Chart.

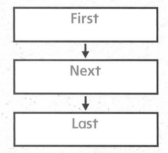

First

↓

Next

↓

Last

Read to Find Out
How does the garden change from the beginning to the end of the story?

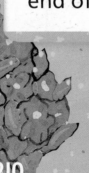

The Ugly Vegetables

by Grace Lin

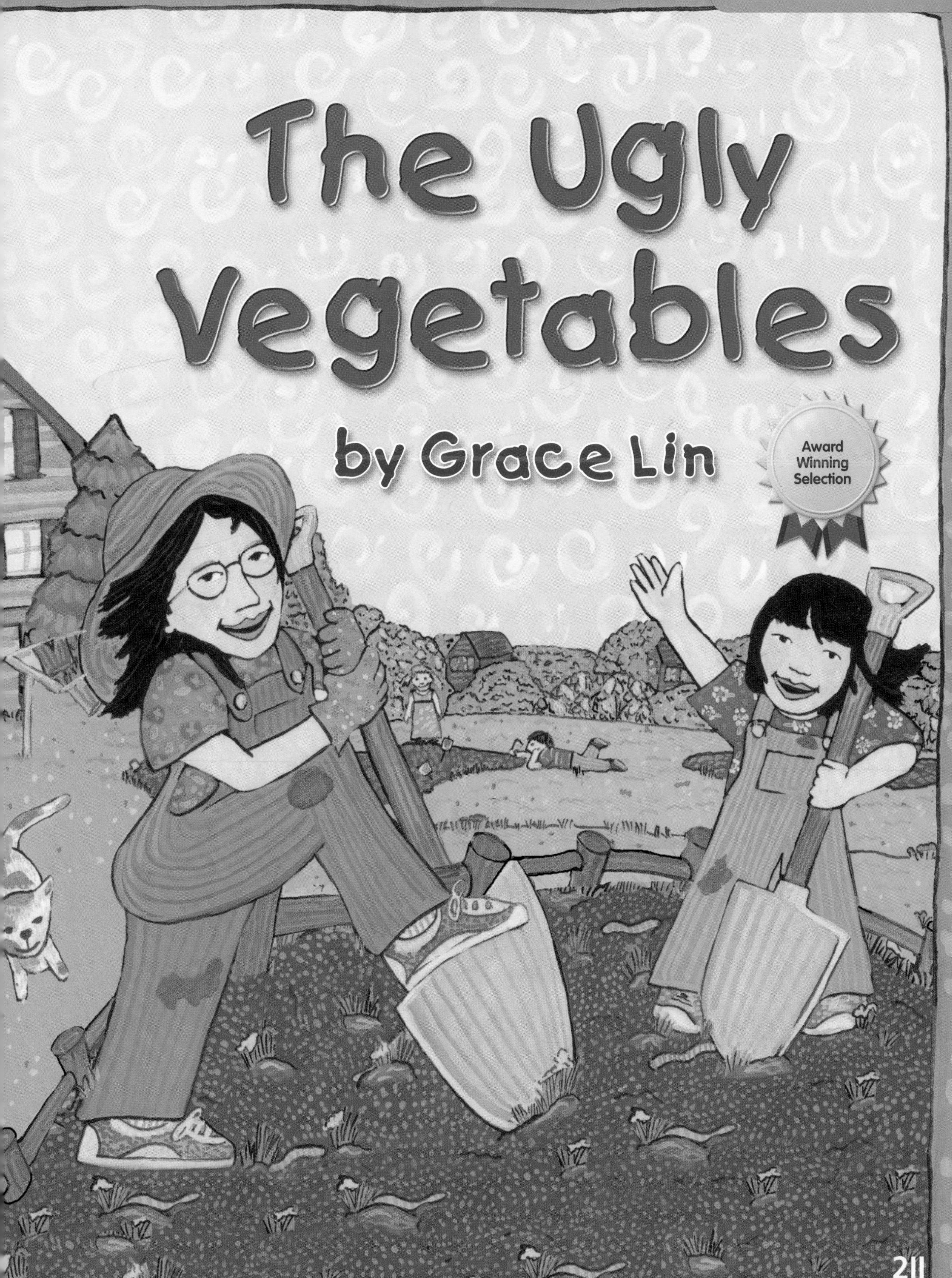

Award Winning Selection

In the spring I helped my mother start our garden.
We used tall shovels to turn the grass upside down,
and I saw pink worms wriggle around. It was hard work.
When we stopped to rest, we saw that the neighbors
were starting their gardens too.

"Hello, Irma!" my mother called to Mrs. Crumerine.
Mrs. Crumerine was digging too. She was using a small
shovel, one that fit in her hand.

"Mommy," I asked, "why are we using such big
shovels? Mrs. Crumerine has a small one."

"Because our garden needs more digging," she said.

I helped my mother plant the seeds, and we dragged the hose to the garden. "Hi, Linda! Hi, Mickey!" I called to the Fitzgeralds. They were sprinkling water on their garden with green watering cans.

"Mommy," I asked, "why are we using a hose? Linda and Mickey use watering cans."

"Because our garden needs more water," she said.

Then my mother drew funny pictures on pieces of
paper, and I stuck them into the garden.

"Hello, Roseanne!" my mother called across the street
to Mrs. Angelhowe.

"Mommy," I asked, "why are we sticking these papers
in the garden? Mrs. Angelhowe has seed packages in
her garden."

"Because our garden is going to grow Chinese vegetables,"
she told me. "These are the names of the vegetables in
Chinese, so I can tell which plants are growing where."

One day I saw our garden growing. Little green stems
that looked like grass had popped out from the ground.

"Our garden's growing!" I yelled. "Our garden's growing!"

I rushed over to the neighbors' gardens to see if theirs
had grown. Their plants looked like little leaves.

"Mommy," I asked, "why do our plants look like grass?
The neighbors' plants look different."

"Because they are growing flowers," she said.

"Why can't we grow flowers?" I asked.

"These are better than flowers," she said.

Soon all the neighbors' gardens were **blooming**.
Up and down the street grew rainbows of flowers.

The wind always smelled sweet, and butterflies
and bees flew everywhere. Everyone's garden was
beautiful, except for ours.

Ours was all dark green and ugly.

"Why didn't we grow flowers?" I asked again.

"These are better than flowers," Mommy said again.

I looked, but saw only black-purple-green vines, fuzzy wrinkled leaves, **prickly** stems, and a few little yellow flowers.

"I don't think so," I said.

"You wait and see," Mommy said.

Before long, our vegetables grew. Some were big and lumpy. Some were thin and green and covered with bumps. Some were just plain icky yellow. They were ugly vegetables.

Sequence of Events
Think about how the garden changes from the beginning of the story until this point. Describe the sequence of events.

Sometimes I would go over to the neighbors' and look at their pretty gardens. They would show the poppies and peonies and petunias to me, and I would feel sad that our garden wasn't as nice.

One day my mother and I picked the vegetables from the garden. We filled a whole wheelbarrow full of them. We wheeled them to the kitchen. My mother washed them and took a big knife and started to chop them.

"Aie-yow!" she said when she cut them. She had to use all her **muscles**. The vegetables were hard and tough.

"This is a sheau hwang gua," Mommy said, handing me a bumpy, curled vegetable. She pointed at the other vegetables. "This is shiann tsay. That's a torng hau."

> **Sequence of Events**
> Describe how the girl's mother prepares the vegetables. Put the steps in the correct sequence.

I went outside to play. While I was playing catch
with Mickey, a magical **aroma** filled the air. I saw the
neighbors standing on their porches with their eyes
closed, smelling the sky. They took deep breaths of air,
like they were trying to eat the smell.

The wind carried it up and down the street.
Even the bees and the butterflies seemed to smell
the **scent** in the breeze.

I smelled it too. It made me hungry, and it was
coming from my house!

When I followed it to my house, my mother was putting a big bowl of soup on the table. The soup was yellow and red and green and pink.

"This is a special soup," Mommy said, and she smiled.

She gave me a small bowl full of it and I tasted it. It was so good! The flavors of the soup seemed to dance in my mouth and laugh all the way down to my stomach. I smiled.

"Do you like it?" Mommy asked me.

I nodded and held out my bowl for some more.

"It's made from our vegetables," she told me.

Then the doorbell rang, and we ran to open the door.

All our neighbors were standing at the door
holding flowers.

"We noticed you were cooking." Mr. Fitzgerald
laughed as he held out his flowers. "And we thought
maybe you might be interested in a **trade**!"

We laughed too, and my mother gave them each
their own bowl of her special soup.

My mother told them what each vegetable was
and how she grew it. She gave them the soup recipe
and put some soup into jars for them to take home.
I ate five bowls of soup.

It was the best dinner ever.

The next spring, when my mother was starting her garden, we planted some flowers next to the Chinese vegetables. Mrs. Crumerine, the Fitzgeralds, and the Angelhowes planted some Chinese vegetables next to their flowers.

Soon the whole neighborhood was growing Chinese vegetables in their gardens. Up and down the street, little green plants poked out of the ground. Some looked like leaves and some looked like grass, and when the flowers started blooming, you could smell soup in the air.

231

In the Garden with Grace Lin

As a girl, **Grace Lin** wanted to be an ice skater. She drew many pictures of herself skating. But when Grace tried to skate, she often fell on her face. Then she looked at the pictures she had drawn. "Maybe I'll be an artist," Grace thought.

Grace says that *The Ugly Vegetables* is based on her childhood. "My mother used to grow Chinese vegetables in her garden while all the neighbors grew flowers. Year after year, I looked with disgust at our ugly garden and asked, 'Why can't we grow flowers?' My mother always answered, 'Because these are better than flowers.' I never agreed, until one day …"

Other books written and illustrated by Grace Lin

LOG ON ▶ Find out more about Grace Lin at **www.macmillanmh.com.**

CA **Author's Purpose**

Grace Lin tells a story about how she changed her mind about something. Think about a time when you had strong ideas about something and then changed your mind. Write about the event and why it was important to you.

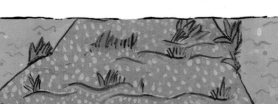

CA Critical Thinking

Retell the Story
Use the Retelling Cards to retell the story.

Retelling Cards

Think and Compare

1. How do the girl and her mother care for the garden? Use details from the story to describe the **sequence of events**. **Summarize: Sequence of Events**

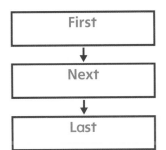

2. Reread page 220. How does the girl feel about her vegetable garden? Why? **Evaluate**

3. What would you like to have **blooming** in a garden—flowers or vegetables? Why? **Synthesize**

4. Why is it important for people to learn about different cultures? **Analyze**

5. Explain why the boy in "City Garden," on pages 208–209, might like the garden in *The Ugly Vegetables*? **Reading/Writing Across Texts**

Genre
Nonfiction gives information and facts about a topic.

Text Feature
Written Directions are steps that tell you how to make or do something.

Content Vocabulary
soil

pottery

directions

California Gardens

Did you know that dirt is not just dirt? California has different kinds of dirt, or **soil**. These soils are used for different things.

Clay soil is red. The red color comes from a mineral called iron. Clay soil does not hold much water so farmers cannot use it to grow many plants. Instead, people use clay to make **pottery**. Clay can be formed into many different interesting and useful shapes.

Clay

234

Some flowers are grown in soil that is mostly sand and shell.

Sandy soil is a light brown color. Not all plants grow well in sandy soil because it does not hold water for very long. Some plants, such as special grasses, do grow well in sandy soil. These plants often grow near the ocean or beaches.

Most plants grow best in topsoil. Topsoil is usually dark brown or black. It has bits of dead animals and plants in it. These nutrients help plants grow tall and strong. Some farmers also use topsoil because it can hold a lot of water. Some flower and vegetable plants need lots of water to grow.

235

You can grow your own vegetables. The directions below will tell you how.

1. Talk to another gardener or to someone at a local nursery. Find out which vegetables grow best where you live. Find out when it is a good time to plant seeds.

2. Dig up the soil where you will plant. Pull out the weeds. Remove any rocks.

3. Rake the soil flat.

4 Poke small holes in the soil. Put a seed in each hole. Cover the seeds with soil.

5 Water the seeds.

6 Check your garden every day.

7 Water the soil when it starts to dry out. Pull out any weeds.

8 Pick the ripe vegetables. Enjoy!

CA Critical Thinking

1. When you are planting a garden, what do you do right after you put a seed in each hole? **Written Directions**

2. Think about this article and *The Ugly Vegetables*. What kind of vegetables would you like to grow? How would you plant these vegetables? **Reading/Writing Across Texts**

Science Activity

Research a vegetable you like. Write a paragraph telling what kind of soil and climate that vegetable needs to grow.

LOG ON ▶ Find more vegetable facts at www.macmillanmh.com

Writing

Sequence of Events

Good writers use **sequence of events** to show the correct order of events in a story.

I tell about the first event at the beginning of my story.

The end tells about the last event in the story.

The Garden Project
by Lydia P.

Mom and I were working in the garden when I remembered my *science* project. "Oh no! I need an idea for my *science* project," I told her. "It's due next week."

"Why don't you think about it while you water the garden?" Mom said.

As I watered the garden, I looked at the different plants in each row. I noticed that the plants had grown since we planted them last month.

I ran over to my mother and said, "My project idea is all *set*. I will show different *seeds* and what the plants look like after they have grown up!"

Your Writing Prompt

A garden can be an interesting setting for a story.

Think about a real or make-believe garden.

Now write a story that takes place in this garden.

Writer's Checklist

 My writing clearly presents a story about a garden.

 The sequence of events in my story is clear, with a logical beginning, middle, and end.

 I use descriptive details to make my story more interesting.

 My sentences are complete and end with the correct punctuation mark. I use pronouns correctly.

How do we learn about animals that lived long, long ago?

LOG ON ▶ Find out more about dinosaurs at www.macmillanmh.com.

ANIMALS LONG AGO

Coelacanth

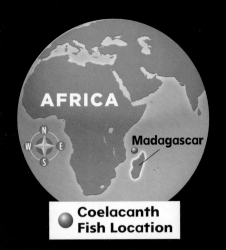

AFRICA

Madagascar

● Coelacanth
Fish Location

A VERY OLD FISH

The coelacanth (SEE-luh-kanth) is an ancient fish. It lived about 360 million years ago. People first learned about the coelacanth by studying its fossils. Fossils are the shapes or remains left behind by something that lived a long time ago.

People believed that the coelacanths died millions of years ago. But in 1938, a fisherman caught a coelacanth near Madagascar. Since then more have been caught. Now scientists are hopeful they can protect coelacanths. They believe they can help because the scientists have learned more about the fish. They know that coelacanths are unable to live in the warm water near the top of the ocean. The fish can only live deep underwater.

242

Scientists made a model of the lizard that lived millions of years ago.

This fossil is the head of the ancient lizard.

BOY FINDS FOSSILS!

In 1999, twelve-year-old Miguel Avelas amazed scientists all over the world. Miguel discovered hundreds of fossils in Patagonia, in the southern part of South America. Miguel led scientists to the **site** where he found the fossils. The scientists guessed the fossils were from a lizard.

The scientists studied the fossils and were able to **confirm** that their idea was correct. The fossils gave them **valid** information that this lizard had lived more than 120 million years ago. Now they also had proof that this lizard had lived in Patagonia. Miguel's discovery gave the scientists important new information.

LOG ON ▶ Find out more about fossils at **www.macmillanmh.com**.

Meet the Super Croc

Did a crocodile the size of a school bus once live on Earth?

What kind of animal was it? Its body was about 40 feet long. That's about the size of a school bus. Its jaws were about 5 feet long. That's about as long as some people are tall! It had about 100 teeth.

Name: *Sarcosuchus imperator* ("Super Croc")
Length: Up to 50 feet
Weight: About 17,500 pounds
Lived: About 110 million years ago

This powerful creature hid in the water, waiting for an animal to come to the river for a drink. Any animal that was grabbed by those teeth would be **unable** to get away.

Don't worry! This toothy giant is no longer alive today. It lived about 110 million years ago, when dinosaurs roamed Earth. That's about 105 million years before human beings were around.

This drawing shows what scientists think "Super Croc" looked like.

Name: Australian crocodile
Length: Up to 23 feet
Weight: About 2,000 pounds
Lived: Alive today

Name: American alligator
Length: Up to 20 feet
Weight: About 1,300 pounds
Lived: Alive today

Paul Sereno shows the skull of "Super Croc."

Paul Sereno, a scientist, was the leader of a team of scientists who found the bones of the animal. They discovered them at a **site** in Niger, a country in Africa.

Sereno and his team were **hopeful** the bones belonged to a kind of giant crocodile from the time of the dinosaurs. But they weren't sure. The whole team needed to study the bones before they could **confirm** their theory. They compared the bones to the bodies of crocodiles living today. If the bones were similar, the theory would be **valid**.

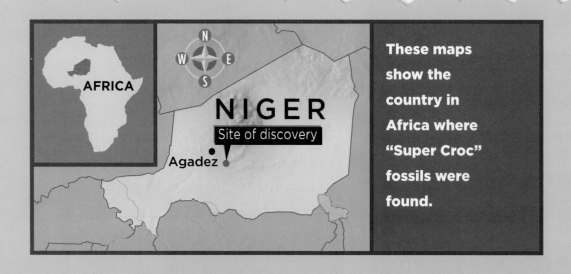

AFRICA

N
W E
S

NIGER

Site of discovery

Agadez

These maps show the country in Africa where "Super Croc" fossils were found.

The shape of the head and skull bones gave Sereno and his team the proof they were looking for. The **ancient** bones belonged to a "Super Croc" that lived at the same time the dinosaurs lived on Earth.

Sereno made copies of the bones to keep in the United States. The original bones were sent back to the country of Niger. If you want to see the real "Super Croc," the bones are on display in a museum there.

A young boy checks out the model of "Super Croc."

CA Critical Thinking

1. How would you summarize this article?

2. How did Paul Sereno prove his theory?

3. If you were a scientist like Paul Sereno, what would you want to study?

4. Compare the creature described in "Boy Finds Fossils!" with "Super Croc." How are they the same? How are they different?

Some Strange Teeth

CA

Show What You Know

Think and Search
Read on to find the answer. Look for information in more than one place.

Scientist David Krause digs for fossils on Madagascar.

Dinosaur fossil hunters were digging in Madagascar. It is an island off the coast of Africa. The team found something that looked like the lower jaw of an animal. It had strange sharp teeth. Was it a dinosaur bone?

"We thought it could be a crocodile or a flying reptile," the team leader said. Scientists studied the hook-shaped teeth. The team discovered that this animal was a dinosaur that lived 70 million years ago and ate fish and insects. For a dinosaur, it was not very big.

Madagascar is a good place for finding dinosaur bones. The oldest dinosaur bones ever found were dug up there. Scientists will keep looking. One scientist said, "We still don't know everything about dinosaurs."

Now answer Numbers 1–4. Base your answers on the article "Some Strange Teeth."

1. **What did fossil hunters find?**
   A the jaw of an old fish
   B the teeth of a crocodile
   C the bones of a flying reptile
   D the jaw of a small dinosaur

2. **What kind of teeth did the jaw bone have?**
   A There were no teeth.
   B The teeth were very big.
   C The teeth could not chew food.
   D The teeth were sharp and shaped like hooks.

> **Tip**
> Look for information.

3. **Why is Madagascar a good place to look for dinosaur bones?**
   A It is very hot.
   B It is far away.
   C The oldest dinosaur bones were found there.
   D Many hunters live there.

4. **Summarize the article about the new dinosaur found in Madagascar. Use details and information from the article to support your answer.**

Write on Demand

Tina wrote a personal narrative about a time when teamwork helped her to find her cat.

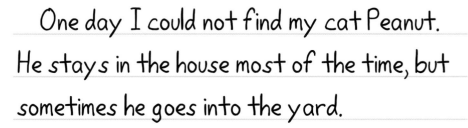

Finding Peanut

My story has a beginning, a middle, and an ending.

One day I could not find my cat Peanut. He stays in the house most of the time, but sometimes he goes into the yard.

Peanut was not in the house. He was not in the yard. I looked all over and called his name. Soon my friend Tracy next door heard me. She said, "Can I help?"

"You go that way," I said. "I'll go this way." I did not see Peanut anywhere.

After a while Tracy came around the corner carrying Peanut! "He was in a tree," Tracy said. "A big dog was barking at him."

I thanked Tracy. I might not have found Peanut without her help.

Your Writing Prompt

Respond in writing to the prompt below. Write for 10 minutes. Write as much as you can, as well as you can. Review the hints below before and after you write.

> Some jobs are too big for only one person.
>
> Think about a time when you worked with a partner or a team.
>
> Write a personal narrative about this time.

Writing Hints for Prompts

- ☑ Think about your purpose for writing.

- ☑ Use interesting nouns and verbs.

- ☑ Write strong paragraphs, with topic sentences and supporting details.

- ☑ Use your best spelling, grammar, and punctuation.

Special Animals

CA **Talk About It**

How do animals change as they get older?

LOG ON ▶ Find out more about special animals at **www.macmillanmh.com**.

253

Leo Grows Up

by Kevin Lee

Leo was a playful kitten. He loved to chase and play with his friends. But sometimes the other kittens weren't nice.

"Look at Leo," they said. "Why is he so big?" The kittens **giggled**. Leo heard their laughs, and it made him sad.

Once a bird **fluttered** by him, flapping its wings as it passed by.

"I wish I was like a bird," said Leo. "I would be light and tiny."

Leo left the kittens. He explored the jungle on his own for many months. Leo grew taller. His fur became thicker.

One day Leo heard a roar behind a bush. He stopped and **peered** over it. When he looked over the top, Leo saw animals that he **recognized**. He knew he had seen them before. They looked just like him, but bigger!

The giant cats ran away. They **vanished** into the trees so Leo couldn't see them anymore. He ran after them. "Look, it's another lion," one of the big cats said.

Then Leo knew why he was bigger than the other kittens. He was a lion, not a cat! That night Leo **snuggled** with the other lions. They slept close together. Finally, Leo belonged.

Reread for **Comprehension**

Ask Questions

✔ Make Inferences

Asking questions can help you understand what you are reading. You can ask yourself questions about what the author tells you and use what you already know to make inferences. Reread the story and use the chart to make inferences about Leo.

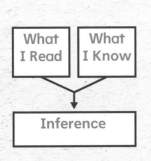

Genre
Fantasy is a story that has made-up characters, settings, or other things that could not happen in real life.

Ask Questions
Make Inferences
As you read, use your Inference Chart.

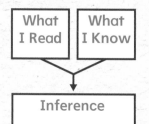

```
┌──────┐  ┌──────┐
│ What │  │ What │
│I Read│  │I Know│
└──────┘  └──────┘
      ↓
  ┌──────────┐
  │ Inference │
  └──────────┘
```

Read to Find Out
How do you know Farfallina and Marcel are good friends?

Farfallina & Marcel

by Holly Keller

Award Winning Author

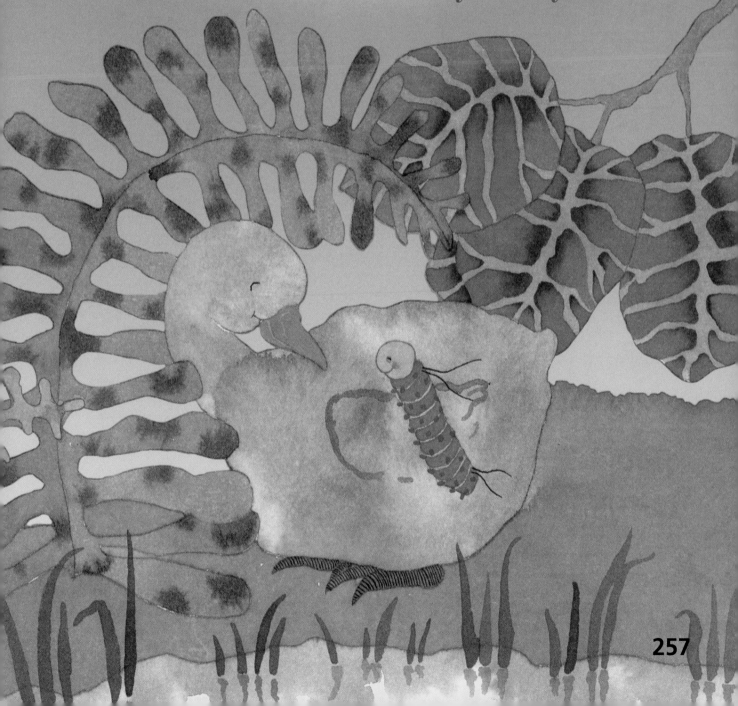

The rain fell all morning.
It splattered on the pond and
splashed on Farfallina's leaf.
She found a dry spot and ate it.
"Hey," said a little voice.
"You're eating my umbrella."
Farfallina **peered** over the edge.
A small gray bird was huddled underneath.

Farfallina liked his soft feathers and his gentle eyes.

"I'm Farfallina," she said,

and she slid down to the ground.

"My name is Marcel," said the bird.

He liked Farfallina's smile and her pretty colors.

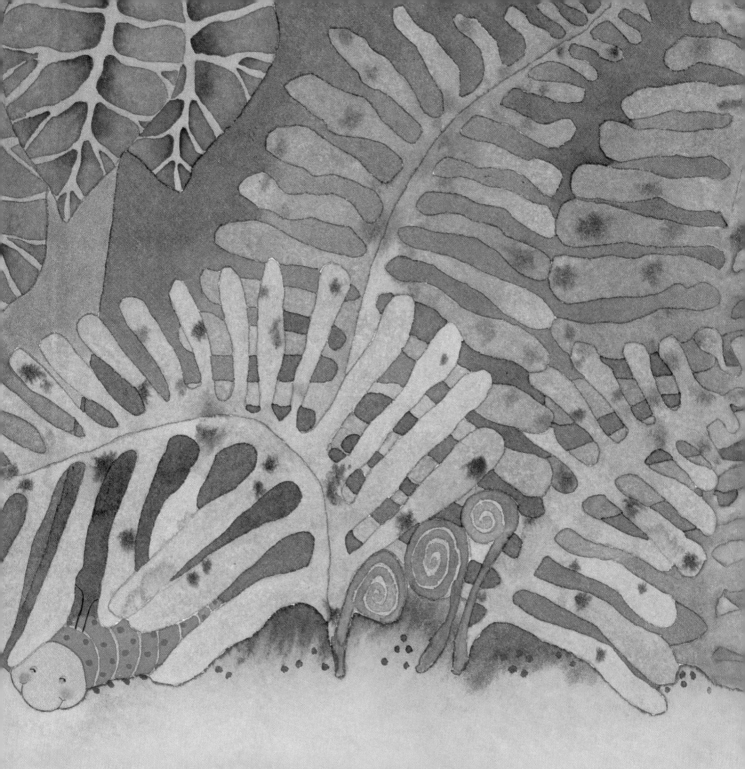

The rain turned to drizzle, and Farfallina wanted to play.

"I'll hide and you find me," she said.

Marcel agreed.

Farfallina hid under a fern close to the ground

because she knew that Marcel couldn't climb.

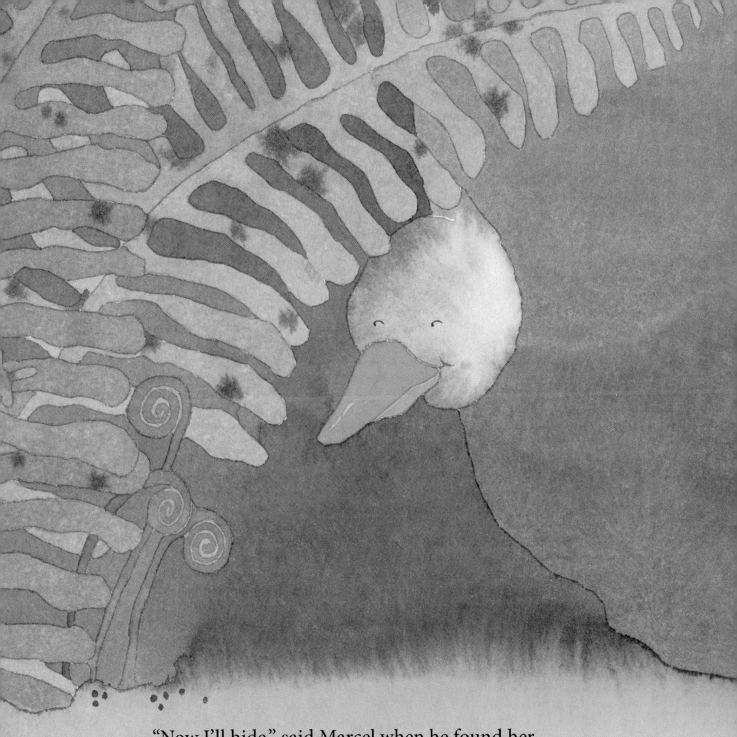

"Now I'll hide," said Marcel when he found her.
And he hid right behind the tree
because he knew that Farfallina moved slowly.

Make Inferences
Use clues from the story to make an inference about the way Farfallina and Marcel feel about each other.

"I can take you for a ride on the pond," said Marcel.

Farfallina inched her way up to Marcel's back.

"You tickle," said Marcel, and he slipped into the water.

Farfallina **giggled**.

"There's so much to see," she said.

Farfallina and Marcel played together every day.

They liked the same games, and they liked each other.

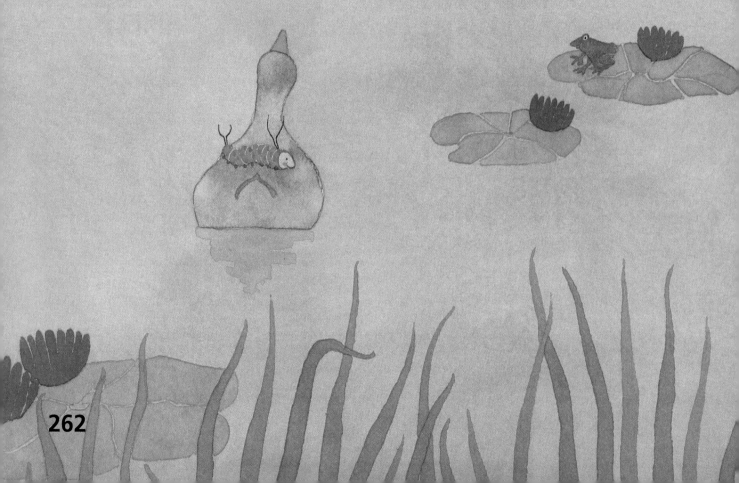

But one day Farfallina was not herself.

"I'm not sick," she told Marcel, "just a little uncomfortable.

I need to climb up onto a branch and rest for a while."

"I'll wait for you," Marcel called as Farfallina made
her way up the tree.

Marcel watched until Farfallina was completely
out of sight. Then he settled himself in the grass
and waited.

Night came and then morning,
but Farfallina didn't come down.
Marcel called to her, but she didn't answer.
He was very worried and terribly lonely.

Weeks went by.
The afternoons grew longer and warmer,
and Marcel went to the pond.

He was growing, and when he looked
at his reflection in the water,
he hardly **recognized** himself.

He went back to the tree every day to look
for Farfallina, but she was never there.
And after a while he gave up.
At the top of the tree Farfallina was **snuggled**
in a blanket of glossy silk.
She was growing too.

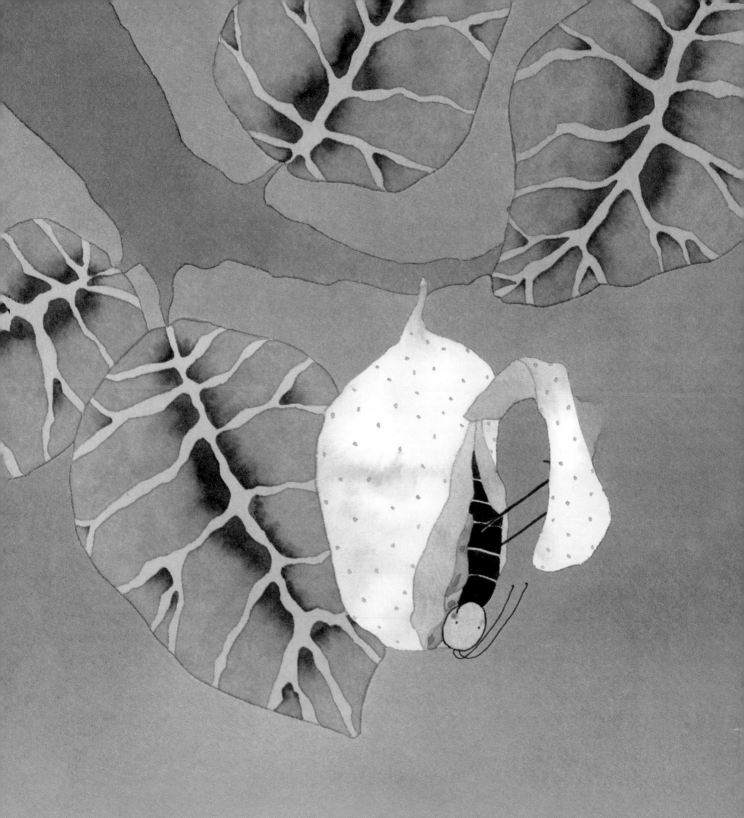

The sky was blue and clear the morning she was ready
to come out and open her beautiful new wings.

She had no idea how long she had been up in the tree,
and she floated down to find Marcel.

"I'll just wait," said Farfallina when she didn't see him,
and she sat on a flower.

Night came and then morning, but Marcel wasn't there.

Farfallina was tired and confused.

She **fluttered** around a bit and went to the pond.

> **Make Inferences**
> Use story clues to make an inference
> about why Farfallina needs to spend
> time alone in the tree.

268

The pond was glassy smooth
except for the ripples
made by a large, handsome goose
who was swimming in solitary circles.
Farfallina shivered with disappointment.

She went to the pond every day to look for the
small gray bird named Marcel, but he never came.
One morning the goose stopped his silent rounds
and spoke to her.
"You must like it here," he said.
Farfallina fluttered a bit.
"I've been waiting for a friend," she said sadly,
"but I don't think he'll come."

Marcel liked her smile and her brilliant colors.

"I know how you feel," he said. "I lost a friend too.

She just **vanished** into thin air."

Farfallina liked his sleek feathers and his gentle eyes.

"A ride around the pond might cheer you up,"

Marcel said.

Farfallina thought it would, and she settled

herself on Marcel's back.

"It's funny," Marcel said, "but I feel as though
I've known you a long time."
"I was just thinking the same thing," said Farfallina.
"My name is Farfallina. What's yours?"

Marcel stopped suddenly.

He beat the water with his strong wings.

Then he swam round and round and round.

"It's me Farfallina," he shouted. "It's me, Marcel!

Is that really you?"

"It is," Farfallina shouted back.

They looked at each other and laughed.

By evening they had explained everything,
and they fell asleep smiling at the stars.

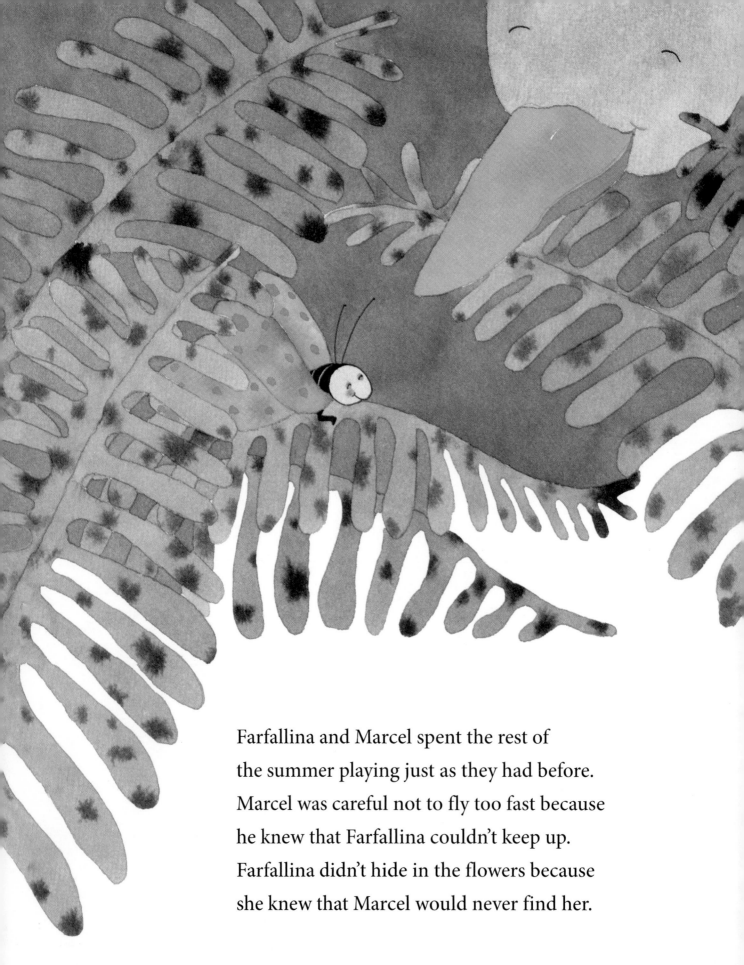

Farfallina and Marcel spent the rest of
the summer playing just as they had before.
Marcel was careful not to fly too fast because
he knew that Farfallina couldn't keep up.
Farfallina didn't hide in the flowers because
she knew that Marcel would never find her.

And when the leaves on the trees
around the pond turned red and gold,
they decided to go south.

Together.

Meet the Author

Holly Keller writes and illustrates books. Her ideas for books come from many places. The idea for *Farfallina and Marcel* started with the word *farfallina*. *Farfallina* means "little butterfly" in Italian. "For some reason," Holly says, "the word caught my fancy."

Other books written and illustrated by Holly Keller

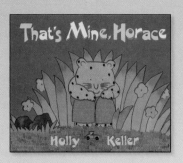

 Find out more about Holly Keller at **www.macmillanmh.com**.

CA Author's Purpose

Holly Keller tells a story about special friends. Write about two good friends. Tell what they do together and why they like each other.

 Critical Thinking

Retell the Story

Use the Retelling Cards to retell the story.

Retelling Cards

Think and Compare

1. Marcel is lonely when Farfallina doesn't return. Use story clues to **make an inference** about why he feels that way. **Ask Questions: Make Inferences**

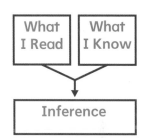

What I Read	What I Know

Inference

2. Reread page 265. Why does Marcel say he hardly **recognized** himself? Use the text and illustration to explain. **Analyze**

3. Would you want a friend like Farfallina or Marcel? Why or why not? **Evaluate**

4. What can you learn about being a good friend from the story? **Analyze**

5. What is similar about the characters in "Leo Grows Up" on pages 254–255 and *Farfallina and Marcel*? **Reading/Writing Across Texts**

Genre
Nonfiction gives information and facts about a topic.

Text Features
Illustrations are drawings that help readers understand information.

Captions explain what is shown in the illustrations.

Content Vocabulary
patterns

stages

hatches

Monarch Butterfly

Butterflies

Butterflies come in all shapes and sizes. Some are big and some are small. Some have bright spots and some have other markings like dark **patterns** on their wings.

The Monarch and the Skipper are two kinds of butterflies. The Monarch is bigger and more colorful than the Skipper. The Monarch is bright orange and black. It has white spots. The Skipper is brown and has clear spots.

Although these two butterflies look different, they have the same body parts as all other butterflies.

280

Butterfly Body Parts

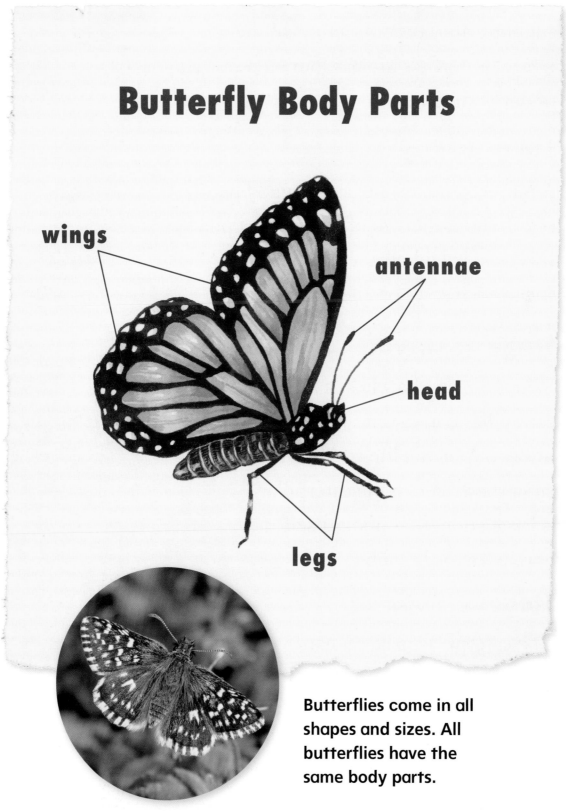

wings

antennae

head

legs

Skipper Butterfly

Butterflies come in all shapes and sizes. All butterflies have the same body parts.

How Butterflies Grow and Change

All butterflies become adults in the same way. Every butterfly's life has four steps, or **stages**, of development.

Stage 1: Egg

A butterfly begins life as an egg. The egg is about the size of the top of a pin. It is usually laid on a leaf. The egg is sticky, so it stays on the leaf.

Stage 2: Larva

When the egg **hatches**, a caterpillar comes out. This part of the butterfly's life is called the larva stage. When the caterpillar is large enough, it hooks itself onto a leaf or branch.

Stage 3: Pupa

The caterpillar makes a hard shell or case to live in. It usually stays inside the shell for a few weeks. This is called the pupa stage. Inside the shell, the caterpillar grows and changes.

Stage 4: Adult

When the shell breaks open, the caterpillar has completely changed into a butterfly. This is the adult stage. After its wings are dry, the butterfly is ready to fly away.

CA Critical Thinking

1. Reread page 281. What is the same about all butterflies? **Illustrations and Captions**

2. Think about this article and *Farfallina and Marcel*. Explain why Marcel does not know who Farfallina is. Use the names of at least three of the stages of a butterfly's life in your answer. **Reading/Writing Across Texts**

Science Activity

Use an encyclopedia to research two types of butterflies that live in your state. Tell how they are alike and different.

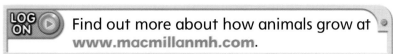

LOG ON ▶ Find out more about how animals grow at www.macmillanmh.com.

283

Reading and Writing Connection

CA **Writing**

✔ **Vary Words**

Good writers vary the words they use to make their writing more interesting.

I use different words to tell about the size of the puppy.

I vary the words here to tell more about how large the dog is.

22 SW 132 Place
Evanston, IL 60060
February 5, 2---

Dear Max,

It was nice to see you at my birthday party. My parents' gift was the best! The puppy they gave me has grown so much. He's huge! At first Murphy slept in my bed. Now he's so big and so heavy that he's sleeping on the floor. Even Murphy's snore is big!

See you soon!

Your friend,
Carlos

Your Writing Prompt

Having something new in your life can be very fun!

Think about when you got something new.

Write about this to a friend.

Writer's Checklist

✓ My writing is a letter that tells about something new in my life.

☑ I **vary the words** that I use to make my writing more interesting.

✓ I include details that give information about what is new in my life.

✓ My spelling is correct. My sentences end with the correct punctuation. I form contractions correctly.

WILD ANIMALS

How do wild animals change and learn to live in their habitats?

LOG ON ▶ Find out more about wild animals at www.macmillanmh.com.

287

Vocabulary

beloved
promised
wiggled
gleamed
glanced
noble

Word Parts

Word Endings added to the end of a verb can tell you when an event took place. The ending *–ed* shows that the action was in the past.

gleam + *ed* = *gleamed*

My Home in Alaska

May 15, 2–––

Dear Katie,

I am so happy to meet my new pen pal! I live in an Eskimo village in Alaska. I live with my parents and my **beloved** grandfather. I love him more than almost anybody!

I want to tell you about going with Grandpa to the tundra near my home. Grandpa had **promised** to show me a wolf. Last Sunday he kept his word.

We got up early. I put on my heavy sweater and **wiggled** into my boots. They were a tight fit so I moved my feet quickly from side to side to get them on.

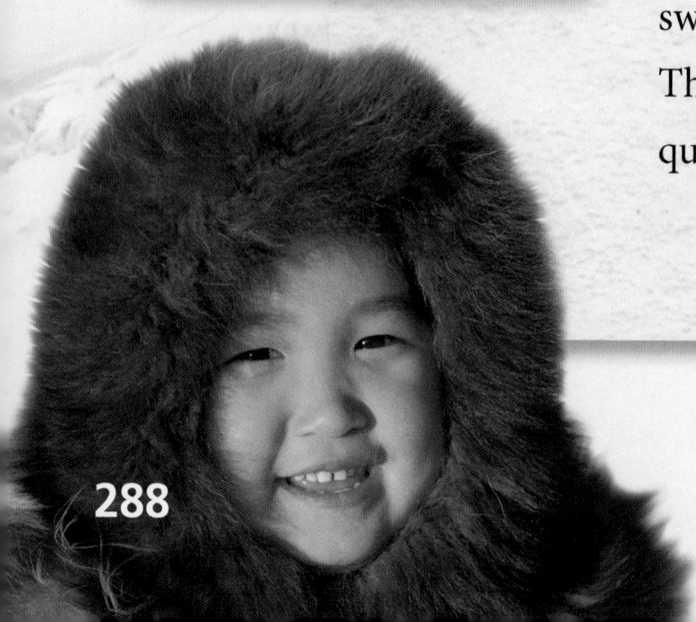

Grandpa and I traveled by dog sled. The snow **gleamed** in the sun. It shone so brightly that we wore sunglasses. We stopped on a frozen lake. Grandpa **glanced** around, looking quickly in each direction. Then his eyes stopped. I looked at the same place. A wolf pack was near the lake. The **noble** wolves stood together. They looked impressive and as proud as kings. I will never forget those amazing animals.

Your new friend,

Jean

Reread for **Comprehension**

Adjust Reading Rate

Make Inferences

Adjusting your reading rate by reading more slowly, along with using what you already know, can help you make a decision, or inference, about a character. Reread the selection and use the chart to make inferences about Jean.

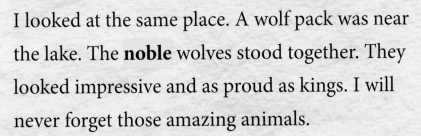

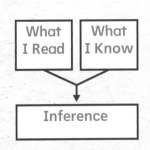

CA Comprehension

Genre
Fiction is a story with made-up characters and events.

Adjust Reading Rate
Make Inferences
As you read, use your Inference Chart.

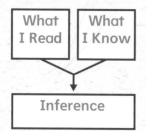

Read to Find Out
How do you know the boy and the wolf pup have a close friendship?

Nutik, the Wolf Pup

by Jean Craighead George
illustrated by Ted Rand

Award
Winning
Author

In an Eskimo village at the top of the world lived a lively little boy. He was not very old, but he could run as fast as a bird's shadow.

When he ran, his father, Kapugen, the great hunter, caught him and lifted him high over his head.

When he ran, his mother, Ellen, caught him and hugged him closely.

When he ran, his big sister, Julie, caught him and carried him home to tell him wolf stories.

She told him how a wolf pack had saved her life when she was lost and starving on the vast tundra. The wolf pack's **noble** black leader had shared his family's food with her.

The wolf's name was Amaroq.

The little boy's name was Amaroq.

One day Julie came home with two pups. They were hungry and sickly. She put one in Amaroq's arms.

"Feed and tend this pup," she said. "His name is Nutik. I will feed and tend the other pup. I named her Uqaq. When they are fat and well, the wolves will come and get them."

Amaroq hugged his pup. He felt the little wolf heart beat softly. He kissed the warm head.

"Amaroq," Julie said when she saw this, "do not come to love this wolf pup. I have **promised** the wolves we will return the pups when they are fat and well."

Amaroq looked into Nutik's golden eyes. The wolf pup licked him and wagged his tail. Julie frowned.

"Don't fall in love, Amaroq," she warned again, "or your heart will break when the wolves come and take him away."

"No, it won't," he said.

Make Inferences
Use details from the story to make an inference about whether Amaroq will begin to love the wolf pup.

Julie gave Amaroq a bottle of milk to feed to his pup. Amaroq wrapped Nutik in soft rabbit skins, and they snuggled down on the grizzly-bear rug.

Every day Amaroq fed Nutik many bottles of milk, bites of raw meat, and bones to chew.

When the moon had changed from a crescent to a circle and back again, Nutik was fat. His legs did not wobble. His fur **gleamed**. He bounced and woofed. When Amaroq ran, Nutik ran.

Summer came to the top of the world. The sun stayed up all day and all night for three beautiful months.

Because of this, Amaroq and Nutik lived by a different clock.

They fell asleep to the gabble of baby snow geese. They awoke to the raspy hiss of snowy owlets.

They ate when they were hungry. They slept when they were tired, and they played wolf games in shadow and sun. They were never apart.

"Don't fall in love with Nutik," Julie warned again when the midnight sun was riding low. "I hear the wolves calling. Soon they will come for their pups." She looked at him. "Be strong."

"I am strong," he answered. "I am Amaroq."

One morning Amaroq and Nutik were tumbling on the mossy tundra when the wolf pack called. They were close by.

"Come home. Come home," they howled.

Nutik heard them.

Uqaq and Julie heard them.

Amaroq heard them. He got to his feet and ran.

Nutik stopped listening to the wolves and ran after him.

Amaroq led Nutik as fast as a falling star. He led him down a frost heave. He led him around the village schoolhouse. He led him far from the wolves.

After a long time he led Nutik home. Julie was at the door.

"Uqaq has returned to her family," she said. "The wolves came and got her. Nutik is next."

"I am very tired," Amaroq said, and he rubbed his eyes.

Julie put him to bed in his bearskin sleeping bag. When Julie tiptoed away, Nutik **wiggled** into the sleeping bag too. He licked Amaroq's cheek.

The sun set in August. The days grew shorter until there was no day at all. Now it was always nighttime.

In the blue grayness of the winter night the wolves came to the edge of the village.

When everyone was sleeping, they called to Nutik.

Nutik crawled out of Amaroq's sleeping bag and gently awakened him. He took his hand in his mouth and led him across the room. He stopped before Amaroq's parka. Amaroq put it on. Nutik picked up a boot. Amaroq put on his boots.

Nutik whimpered at the door.

Amaroq opened it. They stepped into the cold.

The wolves were prancing and dancing like ice spirits on the hill.

Nutik took Amaroq's mittened hand and led him toward his wolf family. The frost crackled under their feet. The wolves whispered their welcome.

Suddenly Amaroq stopped. Nutik was taking him to his wolf home.

"No, Nutik," he said. "I cannot go with you. I cannot live with your family." Nutik tilted his head to one side and whimpered, "Come."

"You must go home alone," Amaroq said, and hugged his **beloved** wolf pup for a long time.

Then he turned and walked away. He did not run. Nutik did not chase him.

"I am very strong," Amaroq said to himself.

He got home before his tears froze.

Amaroq crawled into his bearskin sleeping bag and sobbed. His heart was broken after all.

At last he fell asleep.

Julie awoke him for breakfast.

"I don't want to eat," he told her. "Last night the wolves came and took Nutik away."

"You are a strong boy," she said. "You let him go back to his family. That is right."

Make Inferences
Make an inference about why Amaroq let Nutik return to his wolf pack.

Amaroq did not eat lunch. When Kapugen took him out to fish, he did not fish. Tears kept welling up. He ran home to hide them in his bearskin sleeping bag.

It was surprisingly warm.

Up from the bottom and into Amaroq's arms wiggled the furry wolf pup.

"Nutik," Amaroq cried joyfully. He hugged his friend and **glanced** at Julie. Instead of scolding him, she stepped outside.

"Dear wolves," she called across the tundra. "Your beautiful pup, Nutik, will not be coming back to you. He has joined our family.

"Amaroq loves Nutik. Nutik loves Amaroq. They are brothers now. He cannot leave."

As if listening, the wind stopped blowing. In the stillness Julie called out clearly and softly:

"I shall take care of him as lovingly as you took care of me."

And the wolves sang back, "That is good."

Meet the
Author and Illustrator

Jean Craighead George has written more than 100 children's books.

One summer, Jean went to Alaska to learn more about wolves. There, she saw a little girl walking on the lonely tundra. She also saw a beautiful male wolf. They became the characters for Jean's book *Julie of the Wolves*, for older readers. *Nutik, the Wolf Pup* is a follow-up to that book.

To draw the illustrations for *Nutik, the Wolf Pup*, **Ted Rand** went to Alaska. He wanted to see the tundra for himself. Ted has illustrated more than 60 children's books.

Other books written by Jean Craighead George

 LOG ON ▶ Find out more about Jean Craighead George and Ted Rand at **www.macmillanmh.com**.

CA **Author's Purpose**

Jean Craighead George tells a story about a boy and a wolf pup in an Eskimo village. Think about living in a village like Amaroq's. Would you like it? Explain why or why not.

CA Critical Thinking

Retell the Story

Use the Retelling Cards to retell the story.

Retelling Cards

Think and Compare

1. Julie **promised** the wolves she would return the pups. **Make an inference** about why she lets Nutik stay with Amaroq in the end. Use details from the story to explain. **Adjust Reading Rate: Make Inferences**

What I Read	What I Know

Inference

2. Reread pages 296–297. Why does Julie keep warning Amaroq not to love Nutik? **Analyze**

3. Why does Amaroq let Nutik return to his wolf pack? Would you have let the pup go? Explain why or why not. **Evaluate**

4. Why is it important for Nutik to return to his wolf family and not spend too long with Amaroq? **Analyze**

5. Do you think Jean in "My Home in Alaska," on pages 288–289, and Amaroq might be friends? What are some things that they have in common? **Reading/Writing Across Texts**

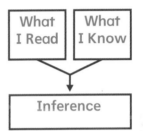

WOLVES

CA Science

Genre
Nonfiction An encyclopedia article gives information and facts about a topic.

✔ Text Features
Encyclopedia entries may have several sections. A Head tells what information is found in each section.

Content Vocabulary
habitats

roam

prey

Wolves are wild animals that are related to the dog family. They look similar to dogs, but they have longer legs and larger feet. They also have more powerful jaws.

Wolves live in different areas, or **habitats**. Some wolves are gray. Others are almost black. Wolves that live in northern Alaska are white. All wolves have long, bushy tails.

Habitat

Wolves live in forest or mountain habitats. Wolves need lots of land because they move around a lot. They **roam**, or travel, 20 miles a day to look for and find food.

Wolves are endangered animals. They used to live all over North America, but now they live only in northern forests and Alaska.

Food

Wolves are hunters. They have a good sense of smell. This helps them find their **prey**. Wolves that live in forests eat mice, rabbits, deer, and moose. Wolves in Alaska also eat caribou or oxen. Finding food is not easy for wolves. Sometimes they must follow a herd for several days. They swallow food in large pieces without chewing. Wolves can eat 20 pounds of meat at one time.

Life Cycle

The female wolf gives birth to pups in the spring. First, she finds or digs a den. Often she will use the same den year after year. The cubs cannot see or hear when they are born. Their mother stays with them for about three weeks. During this time, the male brings food for the mother to eat.

After about a month, the pups can eat meat. All of the pack members hunt food for them. The female hunts, too. Another pack member takes care of the pups while she is away. By fall, the pups have learned to hunt. They are ready to travel with the pack.

Encyclopedia entries often have words in dark print called heads. These summarize what the following section will be about.

The Pack

Wolves live in family groups called packs. A pack may have 7 or 8 wolves. One male is the leader of the pack. He has a female mate. Their children are part of the pack, too. A pack may also have an aunt or an uncle.

CA Critical Thinking

1. In which section would you find information about where wolves live? What did you learn about in the section with the head "Food"? **Heads**

2. Think about the encyclopedia entry and *Nutik, the Wolf Pup*. Write a story about how Nutik's life would have been different if he never left his pack. **Reading/Writing Across Texts**

Science Activity

Research a type of wolf. Write facts about what the wolf looks like and where it lives.

LOG ON Find out more about wolves at **www.macmillanmh.com**.

Writing

A Strong Conclusion

A good writer includes a **strong concluding sentence** at the end of a piece of writing.

My concluding sentence wraps up my report.

I state the title one final time.

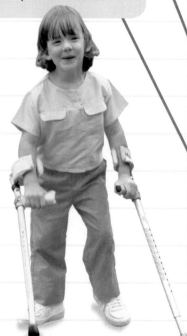

My Book Report
by Jan O.

I really liked Animals of the Sea and Shore by Ann O. Squire. The book describes many animals that live in or near the ocean. Some animals, like whales, live in the water. Other animals live on shore, like snails.

I also learned some unusual facts. Did you know that sea otters sleep floating on their backs? If you like learning about the creatures that live by the water, you'll like Animals of the Sea and Shore.

Your Writing Prompt

A book report gives information
about a book.

Think about a book that you have read.

Write a book report about this book.
Describe why you liked or disliked it.

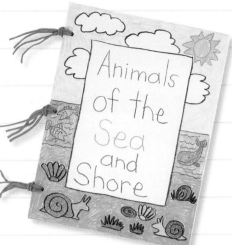

Writer's Checklist

✓ My book report clearly gives information
about a book that I have read.

☑ I include a **strong concluding sentence** to
complete my book report.

✓ I include details that give the reader specific
information about my book.

✓ My spelling is correct. My sentences are
complete. The pronouns and verbs in my
writing agree in number.

✓ **Review**

Draw Conclusions
Sequence of Events
Summarize
Captions
Diagrams and Labels
Homophones

A Birthday Treat

Mom   Dad   Jessie

Jessie's friends

Mom: We are going to the science museum for your birthday today!

Jessie: Hooray! That's my favorite place! Can I invite my friends Ashley, Samantha, and Blake to go with me, please?

Mom: I'm sorry, but I have only two tickets. Also, we need to leave right away. We don't want to miss the volcano movie. Fasten your seat belt. Do you remember where the museum is?

Jessie: Yes. Make a left onto Elm Street. Make a right at the gas station onto Pine Street. The museum is on the right.

Mom: We have 45 minutes before the movie starts. Do you want to look around?

Jessie: Sure! Let's check out the dinosaur exhibit. The dinosaur skeletons reach to the ceiling!

Mom: Before we go, I need to stop at the cafeteria. Let's open the door.

Jessie: What's this?

Jessie's friends: Surprise! Happy birthday!

Mom and Dad: Surprise!

Jessie: Wow! What a great birthday treat!

The Invention of Hook-and-Loop Tape

Did you ever wonder how inventors come up with their ideas? Do they study something closely? Do they work with partners? Or do ideas come to them by accident?

Inventions may begin in any of these ways. Or, they may be the result of them all. That's how it happened for George de Mestral. His invention is hook-and-loop tape. That is the sticky fabric tape that fastens sneakers, caps, and backpacks.

The prickly bur is a seedpod of the burdock plant.

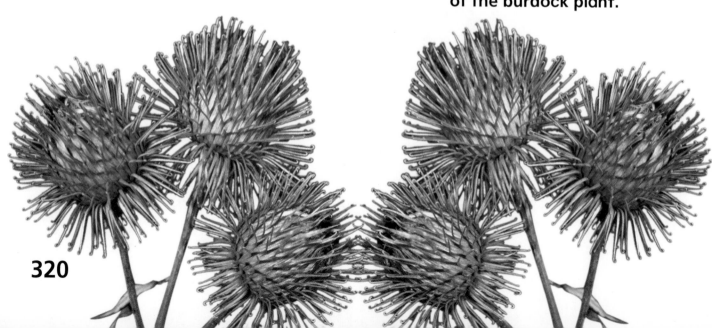

George's idea began when he returned from a walk with his dog. Burs were stuck to his pants and his dog's fur. George pulled them off, but wondered how they held on.

George began to study the burs. What if he could discover the secret of their strong grip? Maybe he could invent a strong fastener.

George's breakthrough came with a microscope. He saw that burs were covered with tiny hooks. The hooks grabbed onto anything with a loop!

Next, George worked with a weaver to make one piece of tape with hooks and another piece with loops. Put together, the pieces imitated a bur.

Today, people use hook-and-loop tape instead of buttons, strings, or zippers.

hook

loop

The hooks attach to the loops in the same way burs grab tightly to fur.

CA Critical Thinking

Now answer numbers I through 4. Base your answers on the story "A Birthday Treat."

I. **Which word is a HOMOPHONE for two?**

   A toot

   B tune

   C pair

   D too

2. **What happens in the MIDDLE of this story?**

   A Jessie and her parents go into the museum.

   B Jessie sees her friends in the cafeteria.

   C Mom asks Jessie for directions to the museum.

   D Jessie watches a movie about a volcano.

3. **Draw a conclusion about why Mom does not let Jessie invite her friends to the museum.**

   A Jessie's friends are too noisy.

   B The friends do not know how to get to the museum.

   C Mom has already invited the friends as a surprise.

   D Jessie's friends do not like museums.

4. **Write a new ending to "A Birthday Treat." Explain how your new ending changes the story's plot and characters.**

Now answer numbers I through 4. Base your answers on the selection "The Invention of Hook-and-Loop Tape."

I. **Which word is a HOMOPHONE for piece?**

A pies   C part

B peace   D whole

2. **What is a bur?**

A the flower of the burdock plant

B a piece of hook-and-loop tape

C the seedpod of the burdock plant

D a bit of sticky tape

3. **What conclusion can you draw about why hook-and-loop tape is helpful?**

A It keeps burs off dogs.

B It is harder to use than buttons.

C It can glue paper together.

D It fastens things without a zipper, buttons, or string.

4. **What event happened FIRST?**

A George de Mestral found burs on his dog's fur.

B George de Mestral went for a walk with his dog.

C George de Mestral studied burs.

D George de Mestral worked with a weaver.

Write on Demand

PROMPT Think of an invention that you use every day. Explain why this invention is useful. Write for 10 minutes. Write as much as you can as well as you can.

The Big Question

How do we learn about nature?

Theme Launcher Video

 Find out more about nature at **www.macmillanmh.com**.

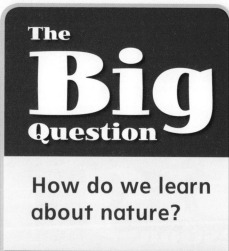

Observing plants and animals helps us learn how they live in different environments. We notice how habitats are different and what animals and plants do to meet their needs in different places. People also use natural resources from the environment. Wood from trees is used to make pencils, water from rivers is used to grow fruits and vegetables, and coal mined from the earth is used as fuel. Learning about these natural resources will help you to preserve the environment so living things have what they need to survive.

Research Activities

Throughout this unit you will gather information about natural resources and the environment. Choose one topic to focus your research on, such as a way to help the planet or the features of a habitat. Create a nonfiction picture book that describes your topic.

Keep Track of Ideas

As you read, keep track of all you learn about the world and its natural resources. Use the Layered Book organizer. On the top flap, write the unit theme. On each layer of the book, write the weekly theme. Inside each layer, write facts you learn each week.

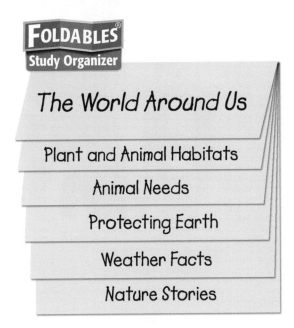

FOLDABLES®
Study Organizer

The World Around Us

Plant and Animal Habitats

Animal Needs

Protecting Earth

Weather Facts

Nature Stories

Research Toolkit

Conduct Your Unit 6 Research Online with:

Research Roadmap
Follow step-by-step guide to complete your research project.

Online Resources
- Topic Finder and other Research Tools
- Videos and Virtual Fieldtrips
- Photos and Drawings for Presentations
- Related Articles and Web Resources

California Web Site Links

 Go to **www.macmillanmh.com** for more information.

California People

John Muir, Preservationist
In the 1800s, John Muir started the Sierra Club. He wanted people to celebrate and preserve the beautiful wilderness in the western part of the country.

Plant and Animal Habitats

CA **Talk About It**

Think about life in the desert. What is it like for plants and animals to live there?

LOG ON ▶ Find out more about habitats at www.macmillanmh.com.

329

Vocabulary

- burrow
- beyond
- warning
- lengthy
- distant

Context Clues

A **possessive noun** shows ownership. An apostrophe (') and *s* are added to a singular noun to make it possessive.

The *ranger's* map fits in his pocket.

The map belongs to the ranger.

THE COATIS OF THE SONORAN DESERT

by Nya Taylor

Coatis (ko-WAH-tees) are animals that live in the desert. They look like raccoons and are about as big as cats. They have long tails that help them balance as they climb.

Coatis like to eat plants and insects. They use their claws to dig for small animals that may be living underground in a **burrow**. Some coatis eat while hanging from trees.

Coatis live together. They do not wander **beyond** their group. Staying close together helps them hear **warning** calls if danger is near. Coatis spend hours taking **lengthy** rests in the shade. During the hot days, they need to stay cool. At night, they climb into trees to sleep.

You can see coatis at the Sonora Desert Museum in Arizona. The park has workers to help you. You may ask to use a ranger's binoculars to see far away. The binoculars will help you spot coatis in the trees in the **distant** mountains.

Reread for **Comprehension**

Summarize

Author's Purpose

One way to summarize an article is to explain the author's purpose. Ask yourself about the reasons why the author wrote this information. Reread the selection and use the chart to summarize the author's purpose.

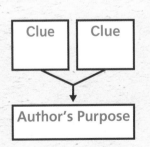

Clue	Clue

↓

Author's Purpose

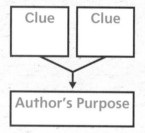
Genre
Fiction can be a made-up story that gives facts about a real topic.

Summarize
Author's Purpose
As you read, use your Author's Purpose Chart.

Clue	Clue

↓

Author's Purpose

Read to Find Out
What do you learn about the toad?

332

DIG WAIT LISTEN

A DESERT TOAD'S TALE

BY April Pulley Sayre

ILLUSTRATED BY Barbara Bash

Award Winning Author

Deep in the desert,
under the sand, the spadefoot
toad waits. She waits…for the
sound of rain.

Skitter, skitter, scratch.
She hears soft sounds.
Is this the rain at last?

No. It's the scorpion overhead,
crawling slowly past.
Skitter, scratch!

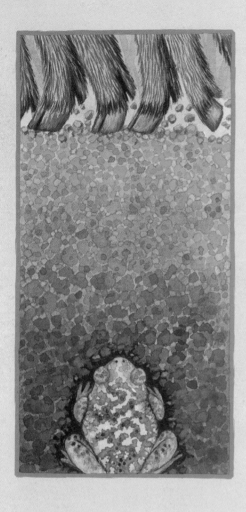

Thunk, thunk, thunk.
Clink, clunk,
clink, clunk.
Sounds shake the soil.

But it's only a herd of peccaries.

Their hooves hammer the ground.

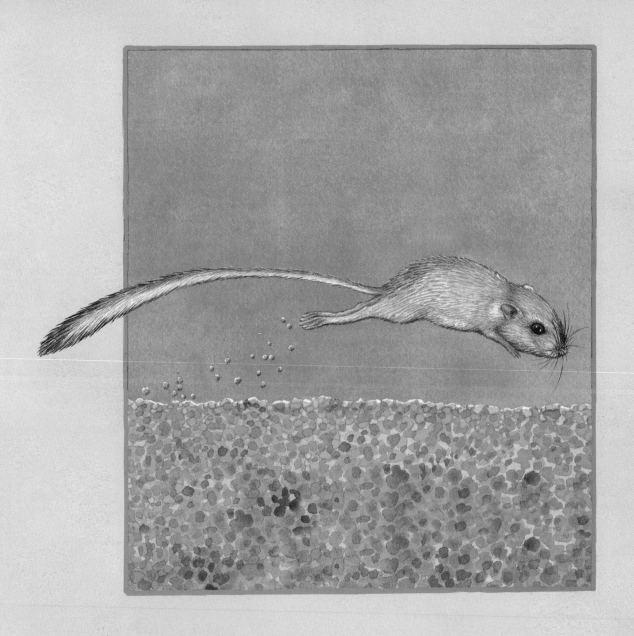

Pop, pop, pop.

What's that sound now?
Is this the rain at last?

No, it's a rat,
hopping in **lengthy** leaps
like a tiny kangaroo.

Will the rain *ever* come?
The desert's so hot, so dry!
And the toad's been waiting
so many months in her
basement **burrow** home.

Why do you think the selection has so much information about the other desert animals? Explain the author's purpose.

338

Tap, tap, tap!

Could this be it?

Is this the rain at last?

No, it's a gila woodpecker

tapping on a tall green cactus.

The toad feels the ground begin to shake.
Then a **crunch, crunch, crunch**
that's loud.
Is this the rain?

No. It's a park ranger's boots
walking on the path.

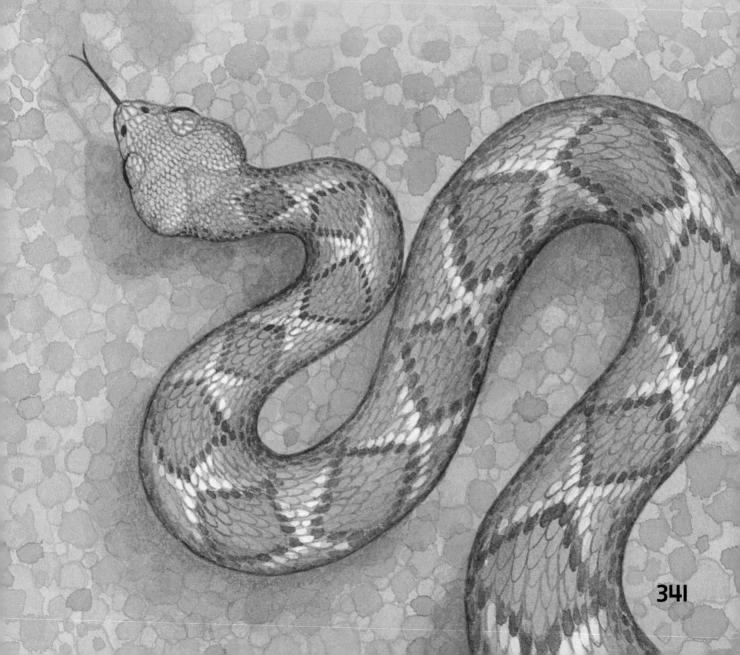

What about that
tsk, tsk, tsk?
Is this the rain at last?

No. It's the rattle of a rattlesnake,
giving warning: STAY AWAY.

Surely that rumbling...
that rumble, rumbling....
Surely that's the rain...?
Not yet.
It's the thunder of a **distant** storm.
But perhaps the rain is near.

Plip, plop, **plip,** plop.
Plip, plop, **plop!**
Is this the rain at last?
Plop **thunk.** Plop **thunk.**
Plop **thunk** *gusssssshhhhhhh!*

It is rain!

The toad hears it.
She digs.

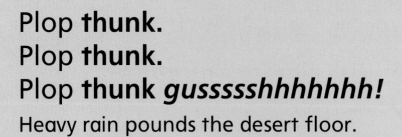

Plop **thunk.**
Plop **thunk.**
Plop **thunk** *gussssshhhhhhh!*
Heavy rain pounds the desert floor.

Push, push, and the toad pops right out, into the open air.

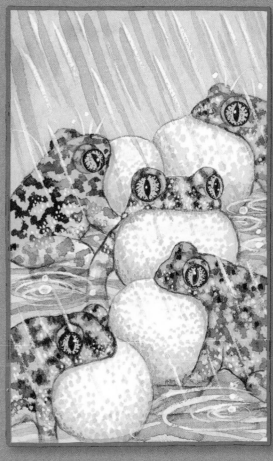

Bleat, bleat, bleat!

The toad hears loud bleats.
Is that the rain sound too?

No. It's male spadefoot toads,
calling: Here, come here!

Plop **thunk**. Plop **thunk**. Plop **thunk** *gusssssshhhhhhh!*

The toad hops in a puddle.
She lays her eggs,
like beads of glass.

Plop **thunk**, plop **thunk**, plop **thunk**
gussssshhhhhhh!

Two days later, the eggs hatch. Wriggling and wiggling in their puddle home, the tadpoles are here at last!

They eat.
They grow.
Legs start to show.
But their puddle is drying up!
Will any make it?

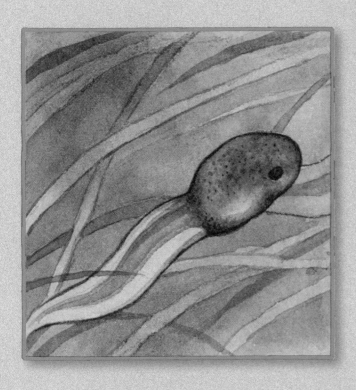

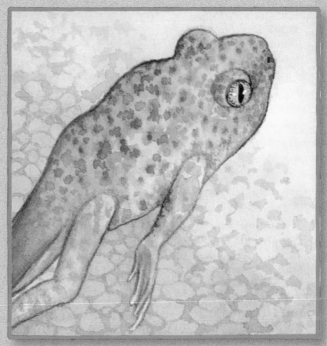

Yes!
With new legs formed,
young toads crawl
from their puddle home.
They rest, then

into the desert **beyond**.

Author's Purpose
Why do you think the author
wrote this story? Explain.

Thump, thump, thump.

Hundreds of tiny toads jump.

The rain has made the desert green.

Yet it won't be long till the desert's dry,
and toads dig down deep with their
spadefoot feet, to wait for that sound...
that marvelous sound,
the sound of the desert rain.

Plop **thunk**, plop **thunk**,

plop **thunk** *gussssshhhhhhh!*

Plop **thunk**, plop **thunk**,

plop **thunk** *gussssshhhhhhhh!*

Plop **thunk**, plop **thunk**,

plop **thunk** **gussssshhhhhhh!**

ENJOY THE OUTDOORS WITH APRIL AND BARBARA

"I love writing—most of the time," says author **April Pulley Sayre**. "Sometimes my first try is horrible. But I rewrite until I like every paragraph. I try to communicate the excitement I feel about nature."

A love of nature also drives artist **Barbara Bash**. When she does research, she uses books and photos to get to know the topic. Next, Barbara visits the places in the stories. "Then," she says, "something alive and personal can be expressed through my books."

Other books written and illustrated by Barbara Bash

  Find out more about April Pulley Sayre and Barbara Bash at **www.macmillanmh.com**.

CA Author's Purpose

April Pulley Sayre teaches readers about desert toads. Think about an animal you know. Write about its life cycle, or all the parts of the animal's life.

354

CA Critical Thinking

Retell the Story
Use the Retelling Cards to retell the story.

Retelling Cards

Think and Compare

1. Why did the author write this story? Use details from the story to describe the **author's purpose**.
Summarize: Author's Purpose

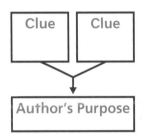

Clue	Clue

↓

Author's Purpose

2. Reread pages 335–337. Why did the spadefoot toad think the noise she heard was rain? What was the noise? **Analyze**

3. Why might it be difficult for some animals to live in the desert? **Analyze**

4. How is a spadefoot toad's **burrow** like other animal homes? **Analyze**

5. How are the coatis in "The Coatis of the Sonoran Desert," on pages 330–33l, and the spadefoot toad in *Dig, Wait, Listen* different? How are they alike? **Reading/ Writing Across Texts**

Genre

Nonfiction

Encyclopedia articles give information and facts about a topic.

Text Features

Charts show information in an organized way. The facts appear in rows and columns.

Content Vocabulary

temperature

adapted

nocturnal

The Sonoran Desert

The Sonoran Desert is a dry area in the American Southwest. It covers about 100,000 square miles in parts of California, Arizona, and Mexico. Some parts of the Sonoran Desert may not have rain for one or two years. Other parts have sudden summer rainstorms more frequently.

Summer in the Sonoran Desert is very, very hot. The **temperature** is often more than 100 degrees during the day. Even in the winter, the temperature is usually above freezing.

Desert plants and animals have **adapted** to life in the desert. They have special ways to survive with very little water and in very hot weather.

Plants

The Sonoran Desert has many different kinds of cactus plants. Cactus plants can live a long time without rain.

Cactus plants store water in their thick stems. They also have thick, waxy leaves that help keep in water. Cactus roots grow close to the top of the ground. When it does rain, the roots can soak up the water very quickly.

357

Sonoran Desert Animals

Name	Type of Animal	What It Eats
black-chinned hummingbird	bird	flowers, nectar, nuts
coyote	mammal	small animals, insects, plants
ground snake	reptile	insects
horned toad	reptile	plants, insects
roadrunner	bird	insects, lizards, snakes
Sonoran Desert toad	amphibian	insects, mice

The animal name is in the first column.

Information about the animal is in the row.

358

Animals

Like desert plants, desert animals can live without much rain. Most desert animals do not have to drink water. They get the water they need from their food.

Many desert animals are **nocturnal**. This means they only come out to find food at night, when it is cool. During the hot days, these animals hide in the shade or underground. Staying cool helps animals keep water in their bodies.

 **Critical Thinking**

1. Which desert animals eat insects? Which desert animals eat only plants? **Chart**

2. Think about this encyclopedia article and *Dig, Wait, Listen*. How is the spadefoot toad like the other animals of the Sonoran Desert? **Reading/Writing Across Texts**

 Science Activity

Use an encyclopedia to research desert plants. Make a chart that gives two facts for each plant.

 Find more desert facts at www.macmillanmh.com.

Reading and Writing Connection

✔ **Important Details**

Good writers use **important details** in their writing. Details tell more about the writer's main idea.

This detail describes the desert heat.

This detail tells the reader how the cactus looks.

June 1, 2---

Dear Cheryl,

How is your summer? Mine has been fantastic so far!

Last weekend, my dad took me to a desert. The air was so hot that it shimmered. The ground was so dry that there were cracks in it! The most amazing thing I saw was a cactus. The cactus was ten feet tall and covered with hundreds of spines. My dad and I had a terrific time.

I will send you pictures soon.

Sincerely,

Maria

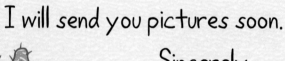

360

Your Writing Prompt

Animals live in amazing places, such as deserts and rain forests.

Think about a plant or animal habitat that you have studied.

Write a letter to a friend that describes this place.

Writer's Checklist

✓ My writing is a letter that clearly describes a plant or animal habitat.

✓ My ideas are grouped together in a way that makes sense and is easy for readers to understand.

☑ There are important details that describe what the habitat looks and sounds like.

✓ My spelling and punctuation are correct. I use interesting adjectives to describe nouns.

CA Talk About It

What do animals
need to survive?

LOG
ON ▶ Find out more about
animals needs at
www.macmillanmh.com.

Animal Needs

✔ **Vocabulary**

beasts
puddles
nibble
itches
preen
handy

✔ **Word Parts**
The **word endings**
–s and *–es* can be
added to make
nouns plural.

beast + s = beasts

Many *beasts* live at
the zoo.

Animals Need to Eat

by Patty Serrano

All animals need to eat, but different **beasts** eat in different ways.

A raccoon searches for fish, nuts, and other things to eat. Raccoons wash all their food before eating it. To do this, they must live near water. Even small pools of water, like **puddles**, will do. After the raccoon washes its food, it begins to eat by taking small bites. The animal may **nibble** on an acorn once it is clean.

A tiger hunts for the meat it eats. Eating can make a mess out of the tiger's fur. There are many places that need to be scratched. To get rid of these **itches**, the tiger bathes in a pond. Later the tiger may lie in the sun and **preen**. It carefully smooths its fur with its tongue.

A spider eats meat, too. It builds a sticky web and then hides. The web is a useful tool for the spider. Bugs get stuck in the **handy** web. Then the spider's dinner cannot escape.

Reread for **Comprehension**

Ask Questions

Compare and Contrast
Asking questions can help you compare and contrast parts of an article. To compare means to tell how things are alike. To contrast means to tell how they are

Animal	Animal	Animal
Behavior	Behavior	Behavior

different. As you reread, use the chart to compare and contrast how the animals in this selection get food.

Genre
Nonfiction selections use photographs and captions to tell about a topic.

Ask Questions
Compare and Contrast
As you read, use your Compare and Contrast Chart.

Animal	Animal	Animal
Behavior	Behavior	Behavior

Read to Find Out
How do the different animals clean themselves?

Splish! Splash!

ANIMAL BATHS

Award Winning Author

by APRIL PULLEY SAYRE

SPLISH! SPLASH!

Take a bath.

Brush your
teeth clean.

And think of
the animals.

They clean
themselves, too.

Squirt!

An elephant sprays
water over its back.

Squirt!!

Baby will get a
shower, too.

Pigs take their baths in thick, brown mud. They soak, slog, snort … and seem to smile. Mud cools their skin. And best of all, it gets rid of **itches**, as well.

Birds take baths in **puddles**. Or shower under sprinklers or waterfalls.

Once clean, they **preen**—
smoothing, fluffing, and
straightening their feathers.
That's like hair brushing for you.

Compare and Contrast
Contrast the ways that
birds and pigs take baths.

Ducks do extra work. They spread oil on their feathers. This special oil waterproofs them. Without it, ducks would get soggy and cold ... which wouldn't be *ducky* at all!

374

Bears have long fur that gets itchy and full of insects.
To scratch itches, a bear rubs against a tree.
Bears also take dust baths. They roll in dirt.
Or they swim and splash in a wide, cool stream.

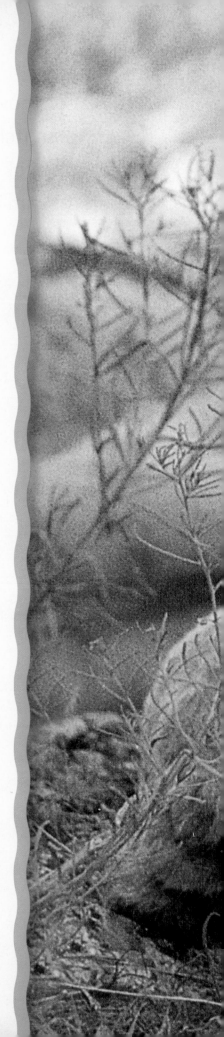

Even the king of **beasts** can get beastly dirty. So lions do what house cats do. They lick their long fur clean. But even a lion's tongue can't reach the back of its head... so it licks a paw and rubs it over its head and ears.

376

A comb might come in **handy** for cleaning a chimpanzee's fur. But chimps don't have combs, so fingers work fine.

Chimps bite and pull bugs and leaves
from their family's and friends' fur.
What are good buddies for?

Oxpeckers, a type of bird, spend their time hanging around. Where? On the bodies of giraffes. Giraffes don't seem to mind. Oxpeckers peck away ticks. They get a meal, and the giraffe gets clean.

Hippos have helpers, too. But these helpers are under water, in the rivers and ponds where hippos wade. Fish **nibble** algae off a hippo's skin. Does it tickle the hippo? Only hippos know. And they won't say.

ish don't take baths. They live in water. But some do try to stay clean. Big fish wait in line—not for a car wash, but for a cleaner fish.

Nibble, nibble, the cleaner fish bites tiny pests off the big fish's scales. The big fish gets clean. The cleaner fish gets a meal. Now that's an amazing deal!

Compare and Contrast
Compare and contrast the ways that some animals get help from other animals to stay clean.

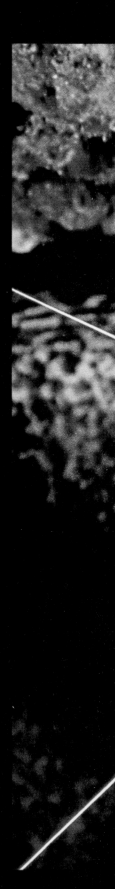

Nearby, a shrimp crawls into a moray eel's mouth.

Will it become a shrimp dinner? Not this time. It's a cleaner shrimp— an animal dentist.

It picks and eats food off the moray's teeth. Instead of being a shrimp dinner, it's dinnertime for this shrimp!

Now that you've heard
about animal baths and animal
dentists, and how animals splish,
splash, peck, and preen ...
it's time to take *your* bath.

Splish and splash.

And think of the animals.
They, too, are getting clean.

Splish! Splash!
April Has Fun on the Job

April Pulley Sayre has written more than 50 books. Many of them are about plants and animals.

"As a child," April says, "I spent hours picking flowers, watching insects, reading books, and writing. Now I do the same thing, only as a career." April's favorite part of the work is researching. She likes reading books and magazines, calling people, and visiting museums, parks, and wild places.

Other books written by April Pulley Sayre

 Find out more about April Pulley Sayre at **www.macmillanmh.com**.

CA **Author's Purpose**
The author explains how animals get clean. Describe what you do to keep clean.

 Critical Thinking

Retell the Selection
Use the Retelling Cards to retell the selection.

Retelling Cards

Think and Compare

1. **Compare and contrast** how the animals in this selection keep clean. Use details from the story to explain your answer. **Ask Questions: Compare and Contrast**

Animal	Animal	Animal
Behavior	Behavior	Behavior

2. Reread pages 378–379. Why might a comb come in **handy** for a chimp? **Analyze**

3. Which animal do you think bathes in the most unusual way? Why? **Evaluate**

4. Why do animals need to keep clean? **Apply**

5. How is "Animals Need to Eat" on pages 364–365 like *Splish! Splash!*? How is it different? **Reading/Writing Across Texts**

Ant and Grasshopper

based on Aesop's Fable

Characters: Narrator, Ant, Grasshopper

Setting: a meadow with an ant hill in the summer.

Scene 1

Narrator: It was summer in the meadow. Most of the insects were working hard to gather food.

Grasshopper: What a beautiful summer day! Ant, why are you working so hard? Come play leaf hop with me!

Ant: I am putting away food for winter so I will not be hungry. I don't have time for playing games.

Grasshopper: Winter is so far away. You have plenty of time!

Ant: Winter lasts as long as summer. You have to be ready! I think you should save some food.

Grasshopper: I'll do it next week. There is no rush.

Narrator: Week after week, Ant worked. Week after week, Grasshopper played leaf hop.

Scene 2

Narrator: Soon winter came. The meadow was covered with snow. There was no food to be found.

Grasshopper: Ant, please help me. I am cold and hungry.

Ant: Oh, Grasshopper, you did not plan. I will give you some food, but next summer you must gather food for yourself.

Narrator: Ant gave Grasshopper some food. Ant also taught Grasshopper an important lesson!

CA Critical Thinking

1. Why is the setting of the play important to the action? **Setting**

2. Think about the play and the selection *Splish! Splash!* How do the animals in both selections meet their needs? **Reading/Writing Across Texts**

LOG ON ▶ Find out more about fables at www.macmillanmh.com.

Reading and Writing Connection

✔ **Strong Topic Sentence**

Remember to write a strong **topic sentence** for each paragraph. A topic sentence tells exactly what the paragraph is about.

① Notes
Chimpanzees, Africa,

② Notes
rocks
sticks

③ Notes
take leaves off the sticks, poke sticks in termite hill, eat insects off stick

Chimps Need Tools
by Jewel W.

Chimps need simple tools to get food. A tool can be something from nature. In Africa, chimps use rocks to crack open nuts. Other chimps use sticks to get and eat termites from termite hills.

The paragraph begins with a topic sentence.

This sentence supports my topic sentence.

392

Your Writing Prompt

All animals have needs.

Think about animals that you know about. Find out facts about one animal's needs.

Now, write a summary about that animal's needs.

Writer's Checklist

✓ My writing is clearly about animal needs.

☑ My summary starts with a strong topic sentence.

✓ I include sentences with details that support my topic sentence.

✓ The punctuation in my sentences is correct. I use the words *a* and *an* in the right places.

Talk About It

How do people cause problems for Earth? What can people do to help?

LOG ON Find out more about ways to help Earth at **www.macmillanmh.com**.

Saving the
World
Around Us

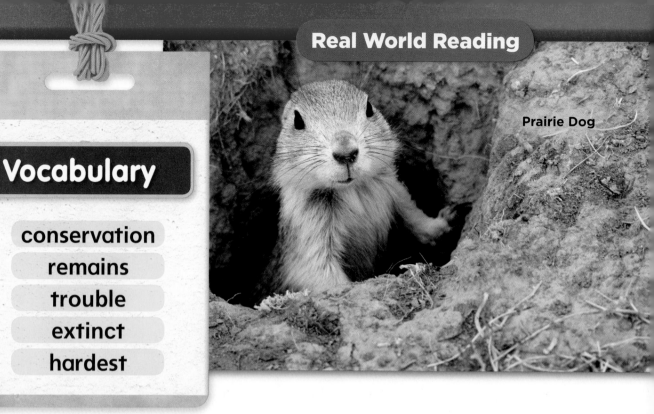

Prairie Dog

- conservation
- remains
- trouble
- extinct
- hardest

Prairie Problem

"We really do not have a lot of time left to save the prairie," says Ron Cole. A prairie is a large, flat area covered with grasses.

Prairies have very few trees. Prairies once stretched across the middle part of the United States. Today, most of that land is covered with farms and towns instead of grasses. Ron Cole belongs to a **conservation** group that teaches people to take better care of the prairie. Their goal is to protect the prairie land that **remains**. That will help the plants and animals that live there.

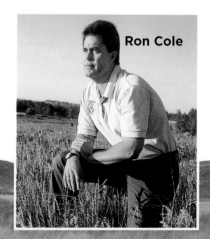

Ron Cole

A South Dakota prairie

396

BE CAREFUL!
WE'RE ALMOST GONE

Experts warn us that many animals on our planet are in **trouble**. More than one thousand animal species are endangered! That means that they may disappear forever and become **extinct**.

It is natural for some plants and animals to become extinct. But now humans are causing more living things to become extinct than ever before. As people cut down forests, mow down prairies, or move into deserts, plants and wild animals get pushed out.

Protecting endangered species is one of the **hardest** jobs people face. The good news is that people are working to solve this problem before it gets worse.

California Condor, an endangered species

Endangered Animals

Amphibians: about 30 species

Insects: about 50 species

Fish: about 130 species

Birds: about 275 species

Mammals: about 350 species

This chart shows the number of animal species that are endangered.

LOG ON ▶ Find out more about endangered animals at **www.macmillanmh.com**.

397

A Way to Help Planet Earth

Plastic bottles are piled high at recycling centers.

What can everyone do to help keep Earth clean?

Keeping Earth healthy is an important job. That's what environmental **conservation** is all about. People who do that job are working to keep the air, land, and water clean. They are also working to keep endangered plants and animals from becoming **extinct**.

One of the **hardest** jobs is solving the problem of trash. The **trouble** with trash is that it keeps piling up. We could run out of places to put it.

A lot of our trash comes from plastic. Soda, juice, water, shampoo—these all come in plastic bottles. Too much plastic is one of our worst trash problems. When a plastic bottle becomes trash, it **remains** trash for hundreds of years. That's because plastic doesn't change much as it gets old.

Is there a better way to deal with plastic? Yes! We can recycle it.

When we recycle, we take something that's been used and turn it into something new. An old plastic bottle can stay old and become trash. Or that old plastic bottle can be recycled and become something new.

People recycle plastic and glass at home and at school.

399

1 Plastic bottles are separated from other trash.

2 Sanitation trucks collect the recyclables.

3 Plastics are taken to a recycling center.

4 Bottles are crushed into small pieces.

Here's how it works. People save their plastic bottles. A special recycling truck picks the bottles up and takes them to the recycling center. Here, the bottles are crushed into small pieces. Then the small pieces of plastic are melted down. The melted plastic is sent to a factory.

At the factory, the old plastic is made into something new. It may become a new bottle or maybe a new rug. It may become a backpack or maybe even a slide at a playground!

5 A factory turns recyled plastic into something new and useful.

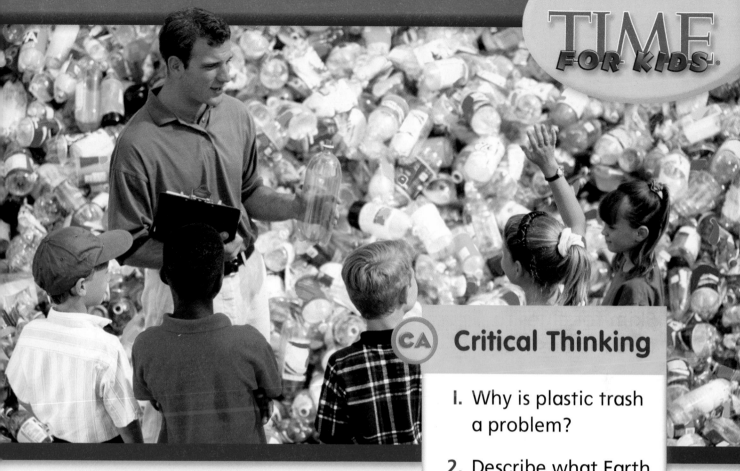

A teacher and students visit a recycling center.

Sometimes there's not much kids can do to help solve our planet's problems. But kids can do a lot about trash. Recycling is one way all people, young and old, can make a big difference!

CA Critical Thinking

1. Why is plastic trash a problem?

2. Describe what Earth would look like without recycling.

3. Besides recycling plastic, what does your community do to help keep Earth clean?

4. Prairies are smaller, some animals are endangered, and too much plastic is being thrown away. How have humans caused these problems?

401

WATER TROUBLES

Show What You Know

Right There
The answer is right there on the page. Skim for clues to find the answer.

These boys in Guatemala are enjoying clean water from a tap for the first time.

Cormelia Gogu lives in Romania. Last year her school did not have clean water to drink because the water pipes were old and rusty. Workers from several countries replaced the pipes so Cormelia's school now has clean water.

Cormelia does not take water for granted. But many people do. In the United States, we can just turn on a faucet to get clean water. It is not that easy in other countries.

Most of Earth is covered with water, but only a small amount is safe to drink. In many places, the water is too dirty to be safe to drink. Other places receive little rainfall, so there is not enough water to grow crops.

Groups such as the United Nations are working to solve these problems. People need to save water so that everyone has enough water to drink.

Go on ▶

CA Standards Practice

Now answer Numbers I through 4.
Base your answers on the article
"Water Troubles."

I. Why is water in many places not safe to drink?

    A It comes from rain.

    B It is too old.

    C It is too dirty.

    D It does not taste good.

Tip
Skim for clues.

2. Why do people need to save water?

    A to keep water clean

    B to help birds and animals

    C so there is enough water to swim in

    D so that everyone has enough water to drink

3. Why don't some places have enough
    water to grow crops?

    A There are too many broken pipes.

    B They receive litte rainfall.

    C There is too much rain.

    D There are too many crops.

4. Describe why Cormelia's school did not have
    clean water. Use details and information from
    the article to support your answer.

Write on Demand

Tom wrote several paragraphs explaining how he would take care of Earth's resources.

We All Need the Earth

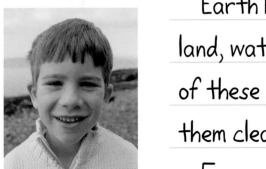

I told my main idea at the beginning of the essay. Then I used details to support it.

Earth has many resources. We have land, water, and air. We need to take care of these parts of Earth. We need to keep them clean.

Farmers use land to grow crops. If we put poison in the ground, crops will not grow. If we put buildings on all the land, there will be no farms. We need to save land.

We all need water. We drink it and use it to stay clean. But people waste water. If we run out of water, we cannot live.

We have to take care of the air, too. We need clean air to breathe. If we stop driving cars so much, the air will be cleaner.

We all need to save Earth's resources.

Your Writing Prompt

Respond in writing to the prompt below. Write for 10 minutes. Write as much as you can, as well as you can. Review the hints below before and after you write.

There are many ways to care for the environment.

Think about what people can do.

Now write an essay about what people can do to keep our land, water, and air clean.

Writing Hints for Prompts

- ☑ Think about your purpose for writing.

- ☑ State your opinion in the topic sentence of a strong paragraph.

- ☑ Support your opinion with details.

- ☑ Be sure you ideas are logical and organized.

405

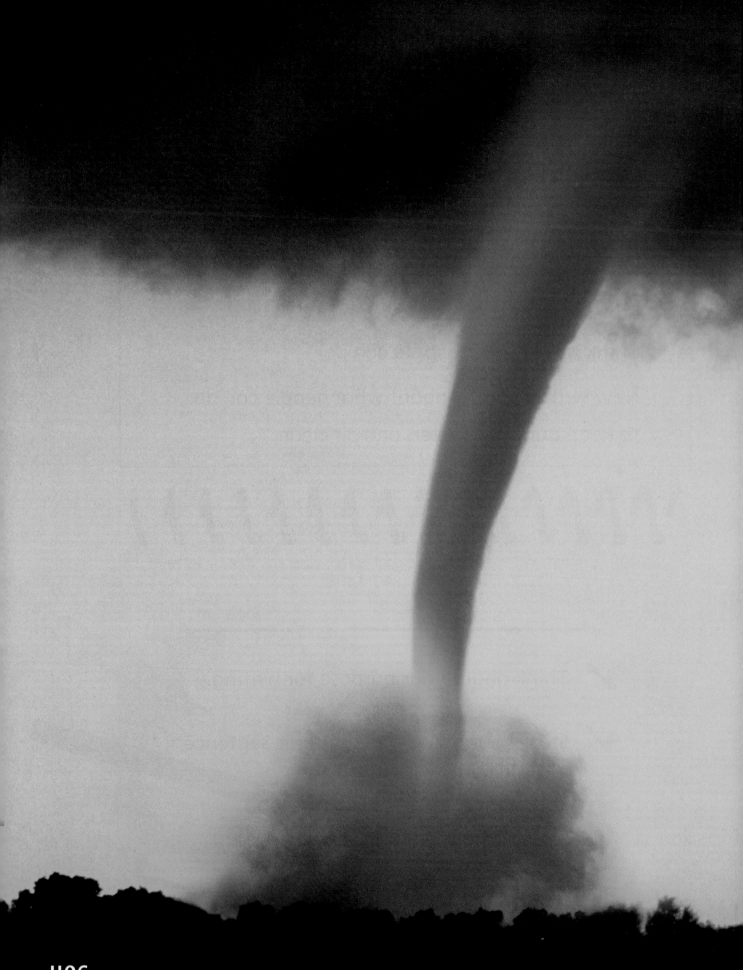

Wild Weather

Hurricane Charley hit Florida in 2004. It was a **violent** storm that caused a lot of damage.

News reports told people in Florida to **beware** of the storm. People had to watch out for heavy rains and strong winds. Some people tried to make sure that their homes were safe. They covered their windows with wooden boards. The boards **prevent** windows from breaking.

Heavy rains dumped water everywhere and caused floods. Powerful winds **uprooted** trees.

408

The trees were blown over and the roots came out of the ground. Strong winds were even able to **destroy** houses. Some were completely flattened. Hurricane Charley also damaged crops. Luckily, it did not hurt any of the cows in the **grasslands**. Farmers took the animals off the grassy fields in time.

Reread for **Comprehension**

Reread

Cause and Effect
Rereading an article can help you identify the causes and effects. An effect is what happens. A cause is why it happens. Reread the article and use the chart to identify the cause and effects of the hurricane.

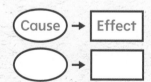

409

Comprehension

Genre
Nonfiction gives information and facts about a topic.

Reread

Cause and Effect
As you read the selection, use the Cause and Effect Chart.

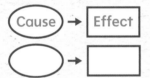

Cause → Effect

Read to Find Out
What is it like when there is a super storm?

SUPER STORMS

by Seymour Simon

Award
Winning
Author

The air around us is always
moving and changing.
We call these changes weather.

Storms are sudden, **violent** changes in the weather.

Every second, hundreds of thunderstorms are born around the world. Thunderstorms are heavy rain showers. They can drop millions of gallons of water in just one minute.

Cause and Effect
What is the effect of a powerful thunderstorm?

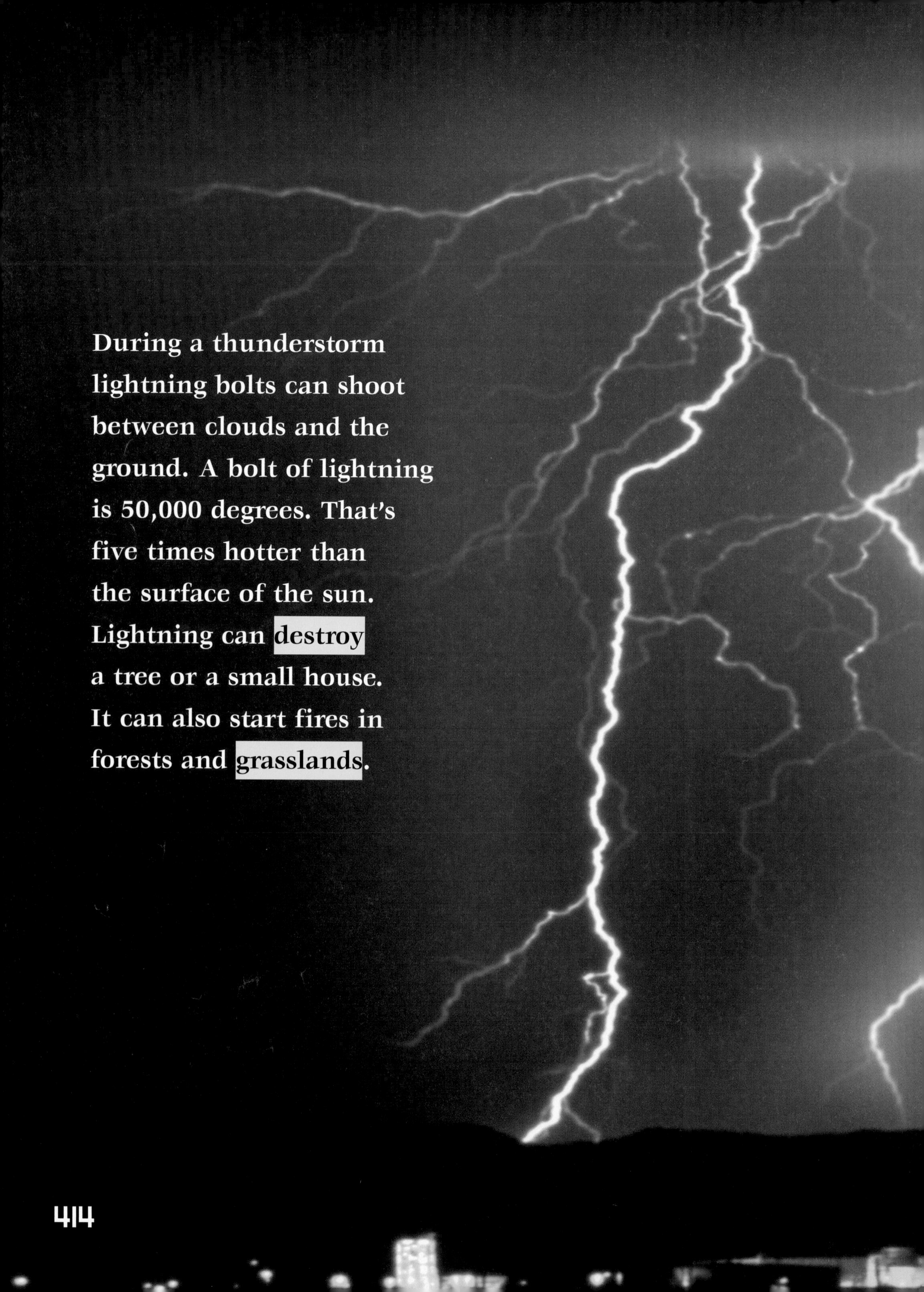

During a thunderstorm
lightning bolts can shoot
between clouds and the
ground. A bolt of lightning
is 50,000 degrees. That's
five times hotter than
the surface of the sun.
Lightning can destroy
a tree or a small house.
It can also start fires in
forests and grasslands.

416

Thunder is the sound lightning
makes as it suddenly heats the air.
You can tell how far away lightning is.
Count the seconds between the flash of
light and the sound of thunder.
Five seconds equal one mile.

Hailstones are chunks of ice that are tossed up and down by the winds of some thunderstorms.

Nearly 5,000 hailstorms strike the United States every year. They can destroy crops and damage buildings and cars.

Hail can be the size of a marble or larger than a baseball.

In July 1995, a fast-moving
group of thunderstorms hit
New York State. Winds reached
speeds of 100 miles per hour.
Over 3,000 lightning bolts
struck in one minute.
And millions of trees were
uprooted or snapped in two.

Thunderstorms sometimes
give birth to tornadoes.
Inside a storm, a funnel-shaped
cloud reaches downward.
Winds inside a tornado can spin
faster than 300 miles per hour.
These winds can lift cars off the
ground and rip houses apart.

More than 1,000 tornadoes strike
the United States each year.
Most of them form during spring
and summer. In April 1974, nearly
150 tornadoes struck 13 states east
of the Mississippi River. More than
300 people were killed and 5,000
were injured. Nearly 10,000 homes
were destroyed.

Television and radio stations often give early alerts. A tornado watch means that one may strike during the next few hours.

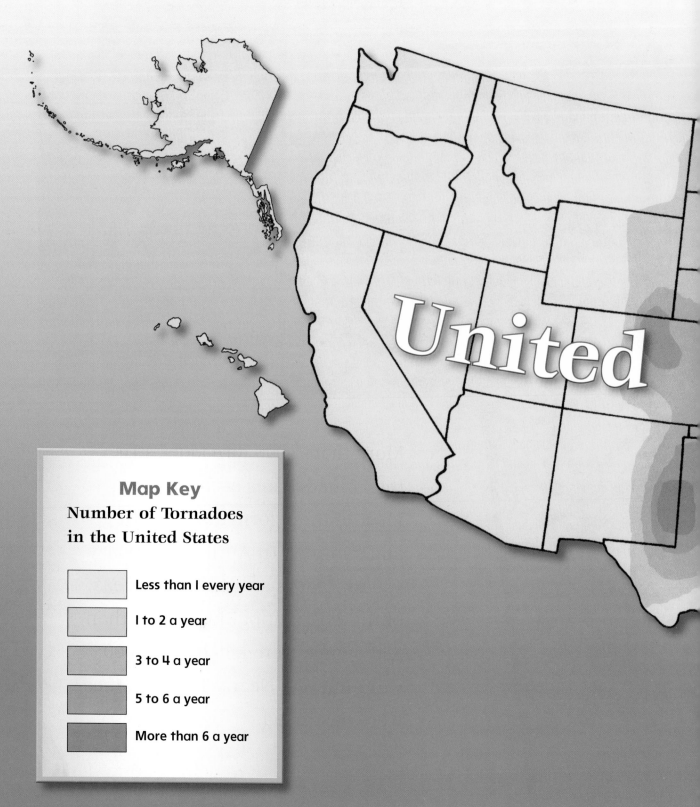

Map Key
Number of Tornadoes in the United States

Less than 1 every year

1 to 2 a year

3 to 4 a year

5 to 6 a year

More than 6 a year

A warning means a tornado has been seen by people or on radar. During a tornado warning you should find shelter in a basement or closet.

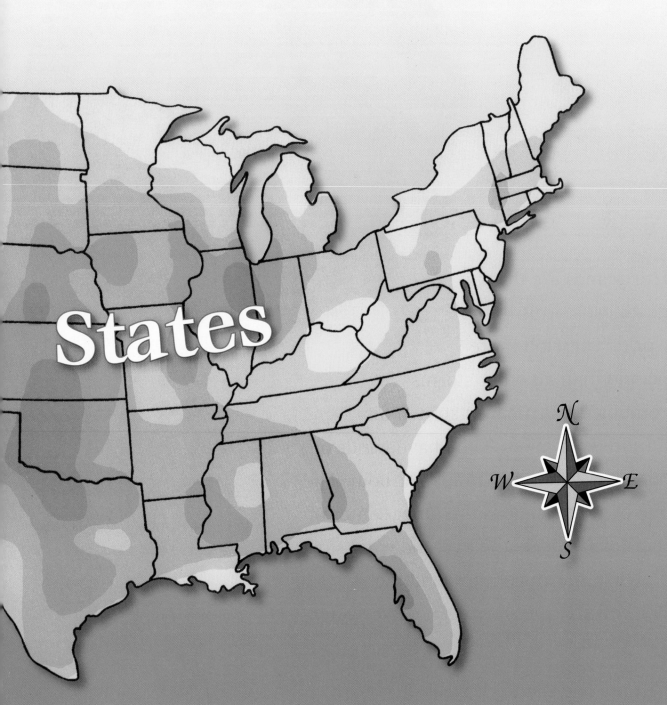

States

The map shows the number of tornadoes that hit the United States every year.

This photograph of a hurricane was taken in space looking at Earth.

Hurricanes are the deadliest storms in the world. They kill more people than all other storms combined. Hurricanes stretch for hundreds of miles. They have winds of between 74 and 200 miles per hour. The eye of a hurricane is the quiet center of the storm. Inside the eye, the wind stops blowing, the sun shines, and the sky is blue. But **beware**, the storm is not over yet.

Cause and Effect
What are the effects of a powerful hurricane?

Hurricanes are born over warm ocean waters from early summer to mid-fall. When they finally reach land, their pounding waves wash away beaches, boats, and houses.

Their howling winds bend and uproot trees and telephone poles. Their heavy rains cause floods.

In August 1992, Hurricane
Andrew smashed into Florida and
Louisiana. Over 200,000 people
were left homeless.

In the Pacific Ocean, hurricanes
are called typhoons. In April
1991, a typhoon hit the country of
Bangladesh. Over a million homes
were damaged or destroyed.
More than 130,000 people died.

Blizzards are huge snowstorms.
They have winds of at least
35 miles per hour. Usually
at least two inches of snow
fall per hour. Temperatures
are at 20 degrees or lower.
Falling and blowing snow make
it hard to see in a blizzard.

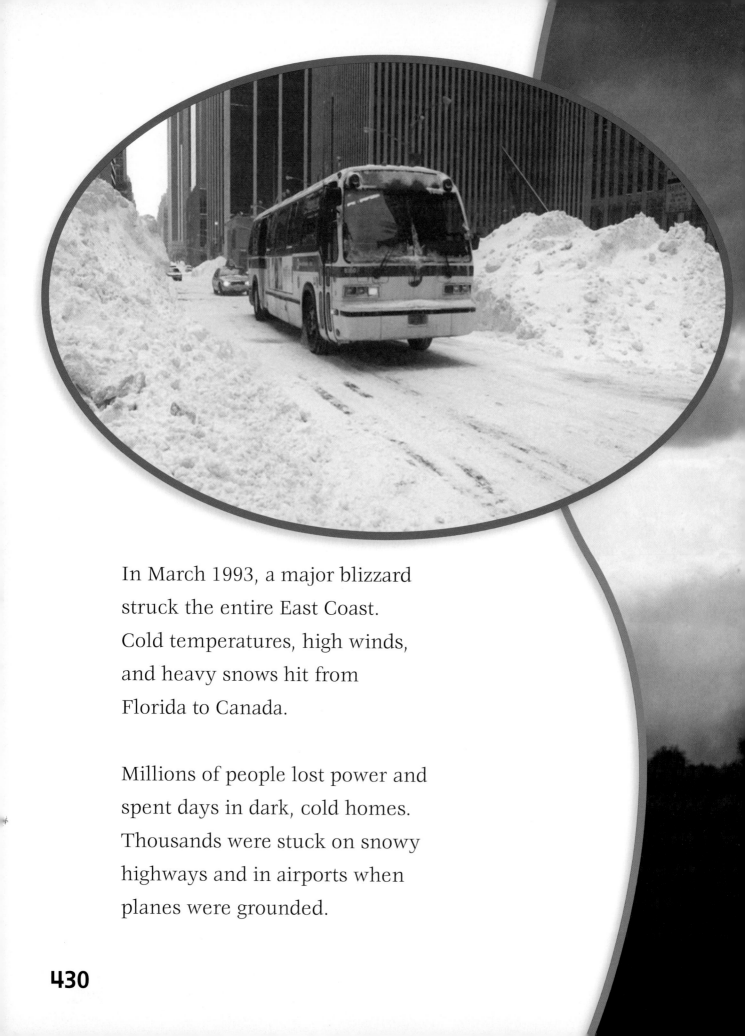

In March 1993, a major blizzard struck the entire East Coast. Cold temperatures, high winds, and heavy snows hit from Florida to Canada.

Millions of people lost power and spent days in dark, cold homes. Thousands were stuck on snowy highways and in airports when planes were grounded.

No one can prevent storms. But weather reports can predict and warn us when a storm may hit. The more prepared we are, the safer we will be when the next one strikes.

Science Facts about Seymour Simon

Seymour Simon has been writing about science for children for more than 40 years. He has written more than 200 books and is working on many more. He says that he'll never stop writing.

Seymour gets his ideas from many places. He says he was always interested in science. For example, Seymour wrote a book called *Pets in a Jar* because he collected little animals in jars as a boy. Other ideas come from his years as a science teacher. Now his grandchildren give him ideas. One grandson asked for a book about trains. *Seymour Simon's Book of Trains* was published soon after.

Other books written by Seymour Simon

  Find out more about Seymour Simon at **www.macmillanmh.com.**

CA **Author's Purpose**

Seymour Simon writes about storms. Think about a big storm that you watched. Write a paragraph that describes this storm.

 Critical Thinking

Retell the Selection

Use the Retelling Cards to retell the selection.

Retelling Cards

Think and Compare

1. What **causes** a tornado? Describe the **effects** of a tornado. Use details from the selection to support your answer.
Reread: Cause and Effect

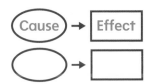

2. Reread pages 424–425. What can you do to **prevent** problems from storms? **Apply**

3. What might happen if a blizzard hit your town? **Synthesize**

4. Why is it important for people to study different types of weather? **Evaluate**

5. What information about hurricanes did you find in "Wild Weather Hits Florida" on pages 408–409 that was not in *Super Storms*?
Reading/Writing Across Texts

Poetry

Genre
Poems can describe a place by using strong words that help form a picture in the reader's mind.

Literary Elements
Repetition is when a word or phrase appears two or more times in a poem.

Word Choice is important in a poem. Poets choose words carefully to give poems a certain feeling or mood.

It Fell in the City

by Eve Merriam

It fell in the city,
It fell through the night,
And the black rooftops
All turned white.

Red fire hydrants
All turned white.
Blue police cars
All turned white.

Green garbage cans
All turned white.
Gray sidewalks
All turned white.

Yellow NO PARKING signs
All turned white.
When it fell in the city
All through the night.

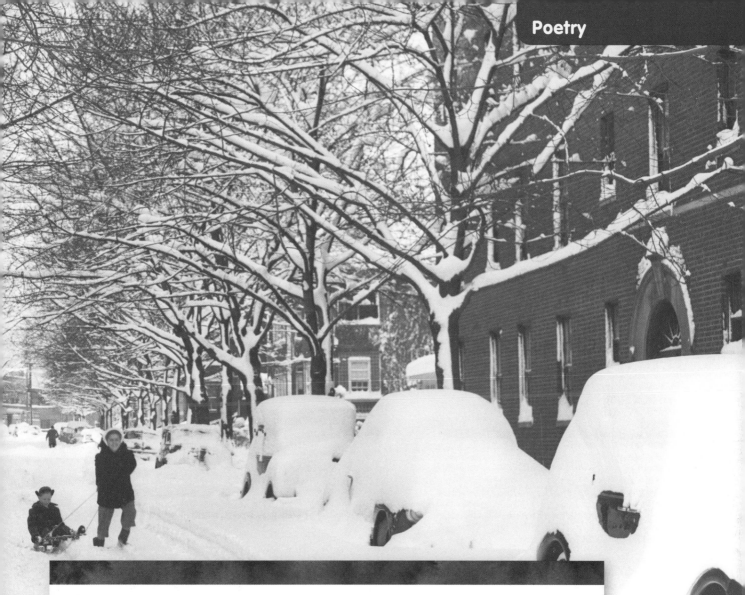

 **Critical Thinking**

1. What phrases are repeated in this poem? Why do you think the author uses so many color words? **Repetition and Word Choice**

2. Think about this poem and *Super Storms*. Which kind of storm is described in this poem? Use details to explain how you know. **Reading/Writing Across Texts**

 Find out more about weather at **www.macmillanmh.com**.

435

CA **Writing**

✓ **Vary Sentences**

Good writers vary their sentence lengths and types so their writing will be more interesting for readers.

I begin my writing with a statement.

I include a question to vary the types of sentences in my writing.

Rain and Snow

by Pedro V.

Rain and snow are kinds of weather. Both give living things the water they need. Did you know that both rain and snow form because of the water cycle? When clouds have too much water, the water falls to Earth as rain or snow. The big difference between snow and rain is temperature. It must be below freezing for snow to fall. If it is warmer than freezing, it rains.

Your Writing Prompt

Everyone has had experiences with weather.

Think about what you know about different kinds of weather.

Write a paragraph that compares two kinds of weather.

Writer's Checklist

✓ My writing is a paragraph that clearly compares two kinds of weather.

✓ I vary the sentence lengths and types to make my writing interesting.

✓ I include details that support the main idea of my paragraph.

✓ I use capital letters and punctuation marks in the right places. I use adjectives that compare correctly.

437

EXPLAINING NATURE

Talk About It

Describe what you can see in the sky. How might people from long ago have explained the natural world?

 Find out more about nature at **www.macmillanmh.com**.

WHY SUN AND MOON LIVE IN THE SKY

Characters

Narrator	Moon
Sun	Water

Scene One: Sun and Moon's house

Narrator: Long ago Sun and Moon lived on Earth.

Moon: Sun, I see a **signal** in the sky. It is a sign.

Sun: Yes, clouds do not take those shapes **randomly**. The clouds do not look that way by accident. Water controls the clouds. I think he is asking me to visit.

Narrator: Sun and Water were friends. But Water never visited Sun and Moon's house.

Scene Two: The next day at Water's house

Sun: Water, please come visit our house.

Water: Your house is too small. I don't fit inside.

440

Sun: Moon and I will build a big new house so you can visit.

Scene Three: Sun and Moon's house

Narrator: Later, Sun told Moon his plan. Moon thought it was a good idea so she **agreed** to help. They decided to build the house with trees.

Moon: I **gathered** the wood and put it all together.

Sun: Please help me carry it. The ends keep **jabbing** and poking me.

Scene Four: Later at Sun and Moon's new house

Narrator: At last, Sun and Moon finished their new house. It was time for Water to visit.

Water: Hello, friends. May I come in?

Narrator: Water entered the house and filled every corner. The house was still too small. There was no room left for Sun and Moon. So, they flew to the sky, where they still are today.

Reread for **Comprehension**

Visualize

✔ **Problem and Solution**

Visualizing, or forming pictures in your mind, can help you understand the problem and solution in a story. Reread the play and use the chart to better understand the problem the characters have and how they try to solve it.

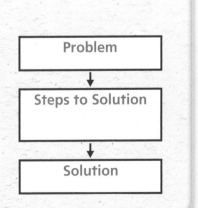

Problem
↓
Steps to Solution
↓
Solution

441

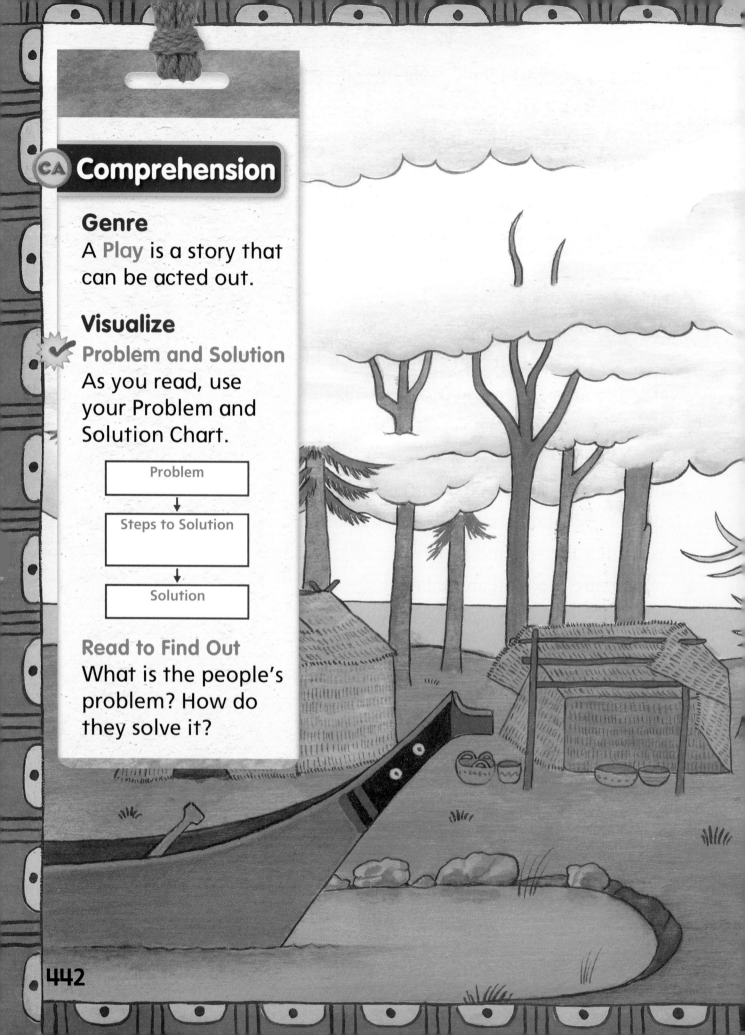

CA Comprehension

Genre
A **Play** is a story that can be acted out.

Visualize
Problem and Solution
As you read, use your Problem and Solution Chart.

Problem

↓

Steps to Solution

↓

Solution

Read to Find Out
What is the people's problem? How do they solve it?

Pushing Up the Sky

BY JOSEPH BRUCHAC

ILLUSTRATED BY STEFANO VITALE

Award Winning Author

SNOHOMISH

The Snohomish people lived in the area of the Northwest that is now known as the state of Washington. They fished in the ocean and **gathered** food from the shore. Their homes and many of the things they used every day, such as bowls and canoe paddles, were carved from the trees.

Like many of the other peoples of the area, they also carved totem poles, which recorded the history and stories of their nation. *Pushing Up the Sky* is a Snohomish story carved into a totem pole in Everett, Washington.

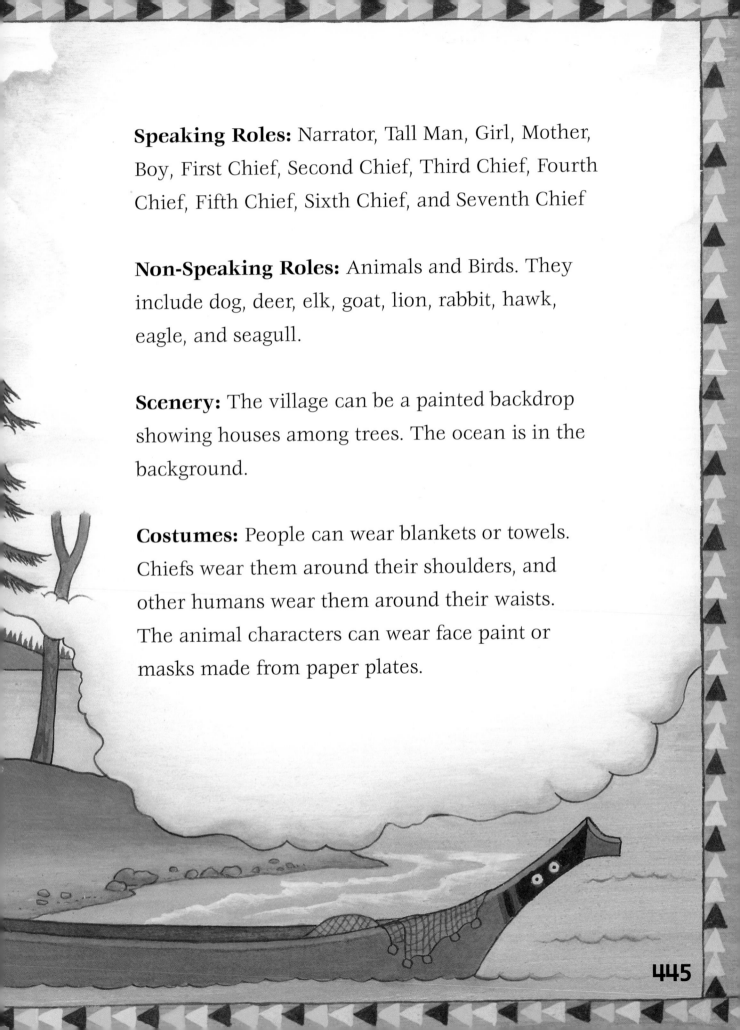

Speaking Roles: Narrator, Tall Man, Girl, Mother, Boy, First Chief, Second Chief, Third Chief, Fourth Chief, Fifth Chief, Sixth Chief, and Seventh Chief

Non-Speaking Roles: Animals and Birds. They include dog, deer, elk, goat, lion, rabbit, hawk, eagle, and seagull.

Scenery: The village can be a painted backdrop showing houses among trees. The ocean is in the background.

Costumes: People can wear blankets or towels. Chiefs wear them around their shoulders, and other humans wear them around their waists. The animal characters can wear face paint or masks made from paper plates.

SCENE 1: A Village Among Many Tall Trees

Tall Man, Girl, Mother, and Boy stand onstage.

Narrator: Long ago the sky was very close to the earth. The sky was so close that some people could jump right into it. Those people who were not good jumpers could climb up the tall fir trees and step into the sky. But people were not happy that the sky was so close to the earth. Tall people kept bumping their heads on the sky. And there were other problems.

Tall Man: Oh, that hurt! I just hit my head on the sky again.

Girl: I just threw my ball, and it landed in the sky. I can't get it back.

Mother: Where is my son? Has he climbed a tree and gone up into the sky again?

Boy: Every time I shoot my bow, my arrows get stuck in the sky!

All: THE SKY IS TOO CLOSE!

SCENE 2: The Same Village

The seven chiefs stand together onstage.

Narrator: So people decided something had to be done. A great meeting was held for all the different nations. The seven wisest chiefs got together to talk about the problem.

First Chief: My people all think the sky is too close.

Second Chief: A very good job was done of making the world.

Third Chief: That is true, but the sky should have been put up higher. My tall son keeps hitting his head on the sky.

Fourth Chief: My daughter keeps losing her ball in the sky.

Fifth Chief: People keep going up into the sky when they should be staying on the earth to help each other.

Sixth Chief: When mothers look for their children, they cannot find them because they are up playing in the sky.

Seventh Chief: We are **agreed**, then. The sky is too close.

All: WE ARE AGREED.

> **Problem and Solution**
> Describe the problem that the characters must solve.

Second Chief: What can we do?

Seventh Chief: I have an idea.
Let's push up the sky.

Third Chief: The sky is heavy.

Seventh Chief: If we all push together,
we can do it.

Sixth Chief: We will ask the birds and
animals to help. They also do not like it
that the sky is so close.

Second Chief: The elk are always getting their antlers caught in the sky.

Fourth Chief: The birds are always hitting their wings on it.

First Chief: We will cut tall trees to make poles. We can use those poles to push up the sky.

Fifth Chief: That is a good idea. Are we all agreed?

All: WE ARE ALL AGREED.

SCENE 3: The Same Village

*All the people, except Seventh Chief, are gathered together. They hold long poles. The Birds and Animals are with them. They all begin pushing **randomly**. They are **jabbing** their poles into the air. (The sky can be imagined as just above them.)*

Girl: It isn't working!

Boy: The sky is still too close.

Fifth Chief: Where is Seventh Chief? This was his idea!

Seventh Chief (entering): Here I am. I had to find this long pole.

Problem and Solution
Why doesn't the first plan to solve the problem work?

452

First Chief: Your plan is not good! See, we are pushing and the sky is not moving.

Seventh Chief: Ah, but I said we must push together.

Fifth Chief: We need a **signal** so that all can push together. Our people speak different languages.

Seventh Chief: Let us use YAH-HOO as the signal. Ready?

All: YES!

Seventh Chief: YAH-HOO.

At the signal everyone pushes together.

All: YAH-HOO!

Seventh Chief: YAH-HOO.

Again everyone pushes together.

All: YAH-HOO!

Tall Man: We are doing it!

Mother: Now my son won't be able to hide in the sky!

Seventh Chief: YAH-HOO.

Again everyone pushes together.

All: YAH-HOO!

Boy: It will be too high for my arrows to stick into it.

Seventh Chief: YAH-HOO.

Again everyone pushes together.

All: YAH-HOOOO!

First Chief: We have done it!

Narrator: So the sky was pushed up. It was done by everyone working together. That night, when everyone looked overhead, they saw many stars in the sky. The stars were shining through the holes poked into the sky by the poles of everyone who pushed it up higher. No one ever bumped his head on the sky again. And those stars are there to this day.

MEET THE AUTHOR AND ILLUSTRATOR

Joseph Bruchac writes stories, plays, poems, and articles for children and adults. He is also a storyteller and performs around the country. Joseph is an Abenaki Native American. All of his work centers on keeping alive the Abenaki culture and that of other Native American peoples.

Stefano Vitale grew up in Italy, where he studied art. Stefano especially likes to create pictures on wood. "There is an ancient quality to wood. It has wisdom and age," he says.

Other books written by Joseph Bruchac

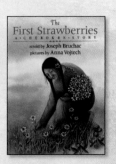

LOG ON ▶ Find out more about Joseph Bruchac at **www.macmillanmh.com.**

CA Author's Purpose

Joseph Bruchac tells a story about people working together. Think about a sport or activity that you do with others. Write a paragraph about how you work together.

CA Critical Thinking

Retell the Story

Use the Retelling Cards to retell the story.

Retelling Cards

Think and Compare

1. What is the **problem** in this play? How is the problem **solved**? Use details from the play to support your answers. **Visualize: Problem and Solution**

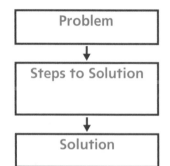

Problem
↓
Steps to Solution
↓
Solution

2. Reread pages 452–453. Why is it important for the people to have a **signal** to push up the sky? **Analyze**

3. Describe how you and your friends or classmates worked together to solve a problem. **Apply**

4. What did you learn from this play about working with others? **Synthesize**

5. How is this play like "Why Sun and Moon Live in the Sky" on pages 440–441? **Reading/Writing Across Texts**

GETTING TO KNOW
JOSEPH BRUCHAC

BY CHRIS LOBACK

Joseph Bruchac is the **author** who wrote *Pushing Up the Sky*. To learn more about Mr. Bruchac, we **interviewed** him. We asked him questions about his work, and he answered them. In this interview the words after **Q:** are the question the interviewer asked. The words after **A:** are Joseph Bruchac's answer.

Q: Why do you write Native American stories?
A: I think that they **appeal** to a lot of people. Children and adults have told me that they like to read them. Native American stories are fun to hear and also teach good lessons.

Q: Why do you write plays?

A: I write plays for two reasons. The first is that many teachers told me it was hard to find good Native American plays for kids. The second reason is that I love to give kids the chance to take part in a story.

Q: Which of your stories do you like the best?

A: My favorites are the stories with monsters and scary events in them. One of these is *Skeleton Man*. I like this scary story because it shows how even a child can beat a monster if she does the right thing!

 **Critical Thinking**

1. What is one reason Joseph Bruchac writes plays? **Interview**

2. Think about this interview and *Pushing Up the Sky*. Do you think this is one of Joseph Bruchac's favorite stories? Explain why or why not. **Reading/Writing Across Texts**

 History/Social Science Activity

Find and read another play by Joseph Bruchac. Perform it with other students.

LOG ON Find out more about plays at **www.macmillanmh.com**.

459

Writing

CA

✔ **Sequence of Events**

Good writers make the **sequence of events** in a play clear by telling the events in order.

The beginning tells what the characters say first.

My ending describes the last event in the play.

 Sun and Wind

by Joe M.

Characters: Narrator, Wind, Sun, Man

Narrator: Wind and Sun are fighting loudly.

Wind: I am stronger than you, Sun.

Sun: No, you're not, Wind. Prove it.

Wind: Do you see that man? Whoever can make him take off his coat is stronger. I'll go first.

Man: Brrrr. The wind is cold. I will button up my coat to keep warm.

Wind: I give up. It's your turn, Sun.

Man: The sun is out. Now it is warm. I will take off this heavy coat.

Wind: You win, Sun. You are stronger.

Your Writing Prompt

A play includes at least one character who speaks.

Think about characters that you might like to write about.

Write a play with characters who speak to one another.

Writer's Checklist

✓ My play includes characters who speak to one another.

☑ My play includes a clear sequence of events.

✓ I include details, such as each character's name, before he or she speaks.

✓ I use the correct punctuation, including a colon after each character's name, when he or she speaks. My adverbs are correct.

✔ **Review**

Author's Purpose
Problem and Solution
Compare and Contrast
Character and Setting
Chart
Compound Words

"Today we're going to use our art materials to make the animals we read about today," Mrs. Baxter told her students. "I want each of you to pick an animal you like," Mrs. Baxter said. "You can use any art materials you want."

There were many good artists in Rico's class, but Rico didn't think he was one of them. "I'll watch how the good artists make animals. Maybe that will help me draw a zebra."

Rico watched Jen drawing an elephant with a marker. Her lines were dark and strong. Her elephant looked great. Rico tried drawing a zebra the same way. But his lines came out too thick and wavy.

Next, Rico walked to Sam's table. Sam was painting a peacock. But when Rico tried to paint the way Sam did, the paint splattered, turning his zebra into a gray mess.

Next to Sam, Rico saw Anna working on a clay crocodile. It had big teeth and a long tail. "I like to work with clay. That's my way," she told Rico.

"Maybe I should stop trying to do what other kids do," Rico said. He got cardboard, colored paper, and glue. He began to work on a zebra model.

"Cool zebra!" said Jen when Rico finished it. "Your model doesn't look like anyone else's!"

Everyone loved Rico's zebra.

"I guess I can be a good artist," Rico said to Mrs. Baxter. "I just have to work my own way."

THE MOTHER OF THE BABY BACKPACK

African mothers can carry their babies everywhere they go.

Have you ever seen a baby carrier? A baby carrier is like a backpack for carrying a baby. Ann Moore introduced the idea of a baby carrier to American people.

Ann was a nurse in Africa in the early 1960s. She saw babies cradled in bright cloth wraps tied to their mothers' backs. This way, the mothers' hands were free to do other things.

In 1964, Ann had her own baby. She tried making a carrier like the one African mothers used. The carrier was like a backpack. Everywhere Ann went with her baby in the carrier, people asked, "Where can I buy one?"

In 1965, Ann and her mother started selling handmade carriers. When the baby carrier appeared in a catalog, many people wanted it.

Ann received a patent for the baby carrier in 1969. By that time, the baby carrier had leg holes and straps that could be made longer or shorter. It could also be worn on the back or front.

By 1979, the baby carriers were made in a factory. More than 25,000 were sold every month. In 1985, Ann sold the company.

Now, all over the world, babies ride in baby carriers, safe and happy, close to their parents.

Ann Moore's baby carriers were very useful to parents.

YEAR	EVENT
early 1960s	Ann Moore is a nurse in Africa.
1964	Ann has a baby.
1965	Ann sells handmade baby carriers.
1969	Ann patents her baby carrier.
1979	Baby carriers are made in factories.
1985	Ann sells her company.

CA Critical Thinking

Now answer numbers 1 through 4. Base your answers on the story "Rico's Zebra."

1. The setting for "Rico's Zebra" is
   A a friend's house.
   B a classroom.
   C Rico's home.
   D a store.

2. What problem must Rico solve?
   A Rico needs to choose an animal to write about.
   B Rico must learn how to paint.
   C Rico has to find his lost markers.
   D Rico has to figure out the best way to create his zebra.

3. The author's purpose for writing this story is to
   A entertain readers with a story about a boy who finds out how to be an artist.
   B entertain readers with a sad story about a zebra.
   C teach readers how to make clay animals.
   D tell readers about different kinds of animals.

4. Think about the story "Rico's Zebra." Think of a new solution to Rico's problem and use it to write a new ending to the story. Explain why your new ending makes sense.

Now answer numbers 1 through 4. Base your answers on the selection "The Mother of the Baby Backpack."

1. Look at the chart. In what year did Ann patent her baby carrier?

   A 1964   B 1965   C 1969   D 1979

2. In the selection, what does <u>handmade</u> mean?

   A made in Africa   C made of cloth

   B made by hand   D easy to make

3. The author's purpose for writing this selection is to

   A explain how to make a baby carrier.

   B teach readers about Africa.

   C make readers laugh.

   D explain how baby carriers were invented.

4. How are the baby carriers in Africa like the ones that Ann Moore made?

   A They were both invented in 1965.

   B They are both made of wool.

   C They are both like backpacks.

   D They are both made in a factory.

Write on Demand

PROMPT Why did Ann Moore invent the baby carrier? Use details to support your answer. Write for 10 minutes. Write as much as you can as well as you can.

Glossary

What Is a Glossary?

A glossary can help you find the **meanings** of words. If you see a word that you don't know, try to find it in the glossary. The words are in **alphabetical order**. **Guide words** at the top of each page tell you the first and last words on the page.

A **definition** is given for each word. An **example** shows the word used in a sentence. Each word is divided into **syllables**. Finally, the **part of speech** is given.

mammal

giggled

Guide Words

First word on the page | Last word on the page

Sample Entry

Definition

Main entry —— **burrow** A hole dug in the ground by an animal. *A gopher lives in an*

Example sentence —— *underground* **burrow**.

Syllable division —— **bur•row** *noun.* —————————— Part of Speech

desert

469

Aa

adapted   Made or became used to. *When he moved to Alaska, he **adapted** to the cold weather.*
a·dapt·ed *verb.* Past tense of **adapt**.

agreed   To have thought or felt the same way as someone else. *My friends all **agreed** it was a good book.*
a·greed *verb.* Past tense of **agree**.

aid   To give help. *I **aid** my grandmother with some household chores.*
aid *verb.*

ancient   Having to do with times very long ago. *Scientists found an **ancient** city buried under layers of dirt.*
an·cient *adjective.*

appeal   To be attractive or interesting. *Does playing a board game **appeal** to you now?*
ap·peal *verb.*

aroma   A pleasant or agreeable smell. *The flowers gave off a wonderful **aroma**.*
a·ro·ma *noun.*

attached   Fastened. *Pedro **attached** this poster to the wall with tape.*
at·tached *verb.* Past tense of **attach**.

attention   The act of watching or listening carefully. *The clown held the children's **attention** with his balloon shapes.*
at·ten·tion *noun.*

author A person who has written a story, play, article, or poem. *Peggy Rathmann is the **author** of Officer Buckle and Gloria.*
au·thor *noun.*

Bb

beasts Animals that have four feet. *Many **beasts** live at the zoo.*
beasts *plural noun.* Plural of **beast**.

beloved Loved a lot. *The class pet was **beloved** by the students.*
be·lov·ed *adjective.*

beware To be on one's guard; be careful. ***Beware** of speeding cars when crossing the street.*
be·ware *verb.*

beyond Farther on. *Look **beyond** the desert and you'll see the mountains.*
be·yond *preposition, adverb.*

blooming Having flowers. *The rose bushes will be **blooming** in June.*
bloom·ing *adjective.*

buddy A close friend. *His **buddy** goes camping with him.*
bud·dy *noun.*

burrow A hole dug in the ground by an animal. *A gopher lives in an underground **burrow**.*
bur·row *noun.*

burst   To break open suddenly. *The bag **burst** because I put too much in it.*
burst *verb.*

Cc

calm   Not excited or nervous. *Because we stayed **calm** during the fire, we got out safely.*
calm *adjective.*

confirm   To show to be true or correct. *Tomorrow's newspaper will **confirm** the report of a fire downtown.*
con·firm *verb.*

conservation   The wise use of the forests, rivers, minerals, and other natural resources of a country. *Water **conservation** is an important issue in many countries.*
con·ser·va·tion *noun.*

Dd

delicious   Pleasing or delightful to taste or smell. *The warm apple pie smelled **delicious**.*
de·li·cious *adjective.*

desert   A hot, dry, sandy area of land with few or no plants growing on it. *Plants that need a lot of water will not grow in a **desert**.*
des·ert *noun.*

destroy   To ruin completely. *A hurricane can destroy a building.* **de·stroy** *verb.*

devoured   Ate or consumed. *The hungry teenager devoured the sandwiches.* **de·voured** *verb.* Past tense of **devour**.

directions   Information or steps to follow about how to do something. *Follow the directions on the package to bake the muffins.* **di·rec·tions** *plural noun.* Plural of **direction**.

distant   Far away in distance or time; not near. *Some of our distant relatives live in Australia.* **dis·tant** *adjective.*

drifts   Moves because of a current of air or water. *When I stop rowing, my canoe drifts along the river.* **drifts** *verb.* Present tense of **drift**.

drowns   To die by staying underwater and not being able to breathe. *A lifeguard watches the pool carefully to make sure that no one drowns.* **drowns** *verb.* Present tense of **drown**.

Ee

enormous   Much greater than the usual size; very large. *Some dinosaurs were enormous compared with animals today.* **e·nor·mous** *adjective.*

examines   Looks at closely and carefully. *The coach always* **examines** *the hockey sticks to make sure they are not broken.* **ex·am·ines** *verb.* Present tense of **examine**.

extinct   When a thing dies out and no more of its kind are living anywhere on Earth. *Dinosaurs are* **extinct**. **ex·tinct** *adjective.*

Ff

fetch   To go after and bring back; get. *Please* **fetch** *two more plates from the kitchen.* **fetch** *verb.*

fluttered   Moved or flew with quick, light, flapping movements. *Moths* **fluttered** *around the light.* **flut·tered** *verb.* Past tense of **flutter**.

force   Strength or power. *Wind can have great* **force**. **force** *noun.*

frantically   Done in a way that is excited by worry or fear. *Maria searched* **frantically** *for her keys.* **fran·tic·al·ly** *adverb.*

friction   A rubbing that can slow things. *When I use my feet to stop my bike, I use* **friction**. **fric·tion** *noun.*

Gg

gas   A substance that spreads to fill a space. *Balloons are filled with air, which is is a kind of* **gas**. **gas** *noun.*

474

gasped   Said while breathing in suddenly or with effort. *"Help!" gasped the struggling child.*
gasped *verb.* Past tense of **gasp**.

gathered   Brought together. *Carol gathered her favorite books to read on vacation.*
gath·ered *verb.* Past tense of **gather**.

gently   Done carefully not to hurt someone or something. *Christopher gently stroked the kitten.*
gen·tly *adverb.*

giggled   Laughed in a silly or nervous way. *I giggled at my mom's funny joke.*
gig·gled *verb.* Past tense of **giggle**.

glanced   Took a quick look. *The driver glanced behind her before safely changing lanes.*
glanced *verb.* Past tense of **glance**.

gleamed   Glowed or shone. *The new bike gleamed in the sunlight.*
gleamed *verb.* Past tense of **gleam**.

grasslands   Lands covered mainly with grass, where animals feed. *Scientists are trying to protect U.S. grasslands.*
grass·lands *plural noun.* Plural of **grassland**.

gravity   The force that pulls things to Earth and keeps them from floating off into space. *Gravity keeps our feet on the ground.*
grav·ity *noun.*

Hh

habitats Places where plants and animals live. *Some of the animals' **habitats** are warm and humid while others are cold and dry.* **hab·i·tats** *plural noun.* Plural of **habitat**.

handy Within reach. *Dad keeps his car keys **handy** in his front pocket.* **han·dy** *adjective.*

hardest Needing or using a lot of work. *My **hardest** chore is cleaning out the garage.* **har·dest** *adjective.* Superlative of **hard**.

hatches Comes from an egg. *The baby bird **hatches** from its egg when it is ready.* **hatches** *verb.* Present tense of **hatch**.

hazards Things that can cause harm or injury. *Ice, snow, rain, and fog are **hazards** to drivers.* **haz·ards** *plural noun.* Plural of **hazard**.

heal To become well or healthy again. *My cut will **heal** after I put a bandage on it.* **heal** *verb.*

hopeful Wanting or believing that something wished for will happen. *We are **hopeful** that the rain will stop before the field hockey game starts.* **hope·ful** *adjective.*

hunger Pain or weakness caused by not eating enough food. *Some wild animals die from **hunger**.* **hun·ger** *noun.*

Ii

informs   Gives information to. *The firefighter **informs** the class about fire safety.*

in·forms *verb.* Present tense of **inform**.

interviewed   To have asked questions to get information. *I **interviewed** the principal for the school newspaper.*

in·ter·viewed *verb.* Past tense of **interview**.

itches   Tickling or stinging feelings in the skin. *Kim rubbed her back to scratch her **itches**.*

itch·es *plural noun.* Plural of **itch**.

Jj

jabbing   Poking with something pointed. *Jason moved his books so they weren't **jabbing** into his side.*

jab·bing *verb.* Inflected form of **jab**.

Ll

lengthy   Being very long in distance or time. *The kangaroo made **lengthy** leaps to cross the field quickly.*

length·y *adjective.*

liquids   Materials that are wet and flow. *Water and juice are examples of **liquids.***

liq·uids *plural noun.* Plural of **liquid**.

Mm

mammal A kind of animal that is warm-blooded and has a back bone. Female mammals make milk to feed their young. Most mammals are covered with fur or have some hair. *My teacher told me that a whale is a **mammal**, but a fish is not.*

mam·mal *noun.*

menu A list of food offered in a restaurant. *Patricia likes to read the whole **menu** before choosing what to eat.*

men·u *noun.*

minerals Something found in nature that is not an animal or a plant. *Salt, coal, and gold are minerals.*

min·er·als *plural noun.* Plural of **mineral**.

muscles Bundles of tissue that move certain parts of the body. *My aunt goes to the gym every day to keep her **muscles** strong.*

mu·scles *plural noun.* Plural of **muscle**.

Nn

neighbor A person, place, or thing that is near another. *A new **neighbor** moved in next door.*

neigh·bor *noun.*

nibble To eat quickly and with small bites. *A mouse will **nibble** cheese.*
nib·ble *verb.*

noble Impressive looking. *The **noble** lion stood proudly at the opening to the cave.*
no·ble *adjective.*

nocturnal Being seen or happening at night. *Owls are **nocturnal** animals.*
noc·tur·nal *adjective.*

normal Having or showing average health and growth. *The doctor said that it is **normal** for a baby to cry.*
nor·mal *adjective.*

Oo

obeys Does what one is told to do. *The dog **obeys** me when I tell him to stop running.*
o·beys *verb.* Present tense of **obey**.

Pp

patterns The way colors, shapes, and lines are placed. *I like **patterns** with dots and stripes.*
pat·terns *plural noun.* Plural of **pattern**.

peered Looked at closely to see clearly. *Carlos **peered** through a telescope to study the stars.*
peered *verb.* Past tense of **peer**.

personal Having to do with a person. *Denise kept her voice low so no one could hear her **personal** information when she was on the phone.*
per·son·al *adjective.*

pottery   Things made from baked clay. *Our art teacher sculpts beautiful **pottery.***

pot·ter·y *noun.*

preen   To make oneself smooth or sleek. *Birds **preen** by washing and smoothing their feathers.*

preen *verb.*

prevent   To keep something from happening. *A seatbelt will help **prevent** an injury in a car accident.*

prevent *verb.*

prey   An animal that is hunted by another animal for food. *Rabbits, birds, and snakes are the **prey** of foxes.*

prey *noun.*

prickly   Having small, sharp thorns or points. *The cactus plants are **prickly**.*

prick·ly *adjective.*

promised   Said that something will or will not happen. *I **promised** that I would clean my room.*

prom·ised *verb.* Past tense of **promise**.

480

puddles Small shallow pools of water or other liquids. *Our driveway has many **puddles** after a storm.*

pud·dles *plural noun.* Plural of **puddle**.

Rr

randomly Made or done by chance, with no clear pattern. *The teacher **randomly** called three students to the front of the room.*

ran·dom·ly *adverb.*

recognized Knew and remembered from before. *I **recognized** my teacher standing in line at the movies.*

rec·og·nized *verb.* Past tense of **recognize**.

remains Things that are left. *The explorers found the **remains** of an ancient building.*

re·mains *noun.*

rescued Saved or freed. *The firefighter **rescued** the cat that had been stuck in the tree.*

res·cued *verb.* Past tense of **rescue**.

481

roam   To move from place to place without somewhere special to go. *The cows roam all over the fields as they eat.*

roam *verb.*

route   A road or other course used for traveling. *We took a different route to the beach because of the traffic.*

route *noun.*

Ss

scent   A smell. *The scent of roses filled the air.*

scent *noun.*

seed   The part of a plant from which a new plant will grow. *We planted a pumpkin seed in the garden to try to grow pumpkins next year.*

seed *noun.*

serious   Dangerous. *The doctor told us that cancer is a serious illness.*

se·ri·ous *adjective.*

signal   A way of showing people to do something. *A red traffic light is a signal to stop.*

sig·nal *noun.*

simmered   Cooked at or just below the boiling point. *The soup simmered on the stove all day.*

sim·mered *verb.* Past tense of **simmer.**

site   A place where something has happened or will happen. *The battle site is just outside the castle's wall.*

site *noun.*

snuggled   Lay close together or held closely for warmth or protection, or to show love. *I snuggled up against my mom during the thunderstorm.*
snug·gled *verb.* Past tense of **snuggle**.

soil   The dirt on Earth's surface. *We dig in the soil to plant flowers.*
soil *noun.*

solids   Firm materials with definite shape. *Rocks are examples of solids.*
solids *plural noun.* Plural of **solid**.

stages   The different steps or times in a process. *During all stages of growth, a flower needs water.*
stag·es *plural noun.* Plural of **stage**.

sunlight   The light of the sun. *We enjoyed the bright sunlight at the beach.*
sun·light *noun.*

swung   Moved back and forth. *We swung back and forth on the monkey bars.*
swung *verb.* Past tense of **swing**.

Tt

temperature   A measure of how hot or cold something is. *You can find the **temperature** by using a thermometer.*

tem·per·a·ture *noun.*

tips   Some helpful information. *My teacher gave me some **tips** for how to spell better.*

tips *plural noun.* Plural of **tip.**

trade   Giving one thing in return for something else. *Swapping an apple for an orange is a fair **trade**.*

trade *noun.*

trouble   A difficult or dangerous condition. *We'll be in **trouble** if we don't complete the work.*

trou·ble *noun.*

Uu

unable   Not having the power or skill to do something; not able. *I was **unable** to reach the light switch because it was too high.*

un·a·ble *adjective.*

uprooted   Torn or pulled up by the roots. *A bulldozer **uprooted** trees and bushes.*

up·rooted *verb.* Past tense of **uproot.**

Vv

valid   Correct based on facts or proof. *My experiment proved that my theory was **valid**.*
val·id *adjective.*

vanished   Gone from sight. *The moon **vanished** behind the clouds.*
van·ished *verb.* Past tense of **vanish**.

violent   Happening with or because of a strong force. *The **violent** earthquake destroyed many homes.*
vi·o·lent *adjective.*

Ww

warning   Notice about a danger. *The sign was a **warning** that the road curved sharply ahead.*
warn·ing *noun.*

wiggled   Moved from side to side in short, sudden movements. *I **wiggled** my loose tooth.*
wig·gled *verb.* Past tense of **wiggle**.

Yy

young   Not old. *A "joey" is what we call a **young** kangaroo.*
young *adjective.*

Acknowledgments

The publisher gratefully acknowledges permission to reprint the following copyrighted materials:

"Dig Wait Listen: A Desert Toad's Tale" by April Pulley Sayre, illustrated by Barbara Bash. Text copyright © 2001 by April Pulley Sayre. Illustrations copyright © 2001 by Barbara Bash. Reprinted by permission of HarperCollins Publishers.

"Farfallina and Marcel" by Holly Keller. Copyright © 2002 by Holly Keller. Reprinted with permission from Greenwillow Books, an imprint of HarperCollins Publishers.

"A Harbor Seal Pup Grows Up" by Joan Hewett and Richard Hewett. Text copyright © 2002 by Joan Hewett. Photographs copyright © 2002 by Richard Hewett. Reprinted with permission from Carolrhoda Books, Inc., a division of Lerner Publishing Group.

"Head, Body, Legs: A Story from Liberia" by Won-Ldy Paye and Margaret H. Lippert, illustrated by Julie Paschkis. Text copyright © 2002 by Won-Ldy Paye and Margaret H. Lippert. Illustrations copyright © 2002 by Julie Paschkis. Reprinted with permission from Henry Holt and Company, LLC.

"It Fell in the City" from BLACKBERRY INK by Eve Merriam. Text copyright © 1985 by Eve Merriam. Reprinted by permission of William Morrow and Company.

"Mice and Beans" by Pam Muñoz Ryan, illustrated by Joe Cepeda. Text copyright © 2001 by Pam Muñoz Ryan. Illustrations copyright © 2001 by Joe Cepeda. Reprinted by permission of Scholastic Press, a division of Scholastic Inc.

"Nutik, the Wolf Pup" by Jean Craighead George, illustrated by Ted Rand. Text copyright © 2001 by Julie Productions, Inc. Illustrations copyright © 2001 by Ted Rand. Reprinted with permission from HarperCollins Publishers.

"Officer Buckle and Gloria" by Peggy Rathmann. Text and illustrations copyright © 1995 by Peggy Rathmann. Reprinted with permission from G.P. Putnam's Sons, a division of Penguin Putnam Books for Young Readers.

"The Puppy" from RING A RING O' ROSES: FINGER PLAYS FOR PRESCHOOL CHILDREN. Reprinted with permission from Flint Public Library.

"Pushing Up The Sky" from PUSHING UP THE SKY by Joseph Bruchac. Text copyright © 2000 by Joseph Bruchac. Reprinted by permission of Penguin Putnam Books for Young Readers.

"Splish! Splash! Animal Baths" by April Pulley Sayre. Copyright © 2000 by April Pulley Sayre. Reprinted by permission of The Millbrook Press, Inc.

"Super Storms" by Seymour Simon. Text copyright © 2002 by Seymour Simon. Reprinted by permission of SeaStar Books, a division of North-South Books, Inc.

"The Tiny Seed" by Eric Carle. Copyright © 1987 by Eric Carle Corp. Reprinted with permission from Aladdin Paperbacks, an imprint of Simon & Schuster Children's Publishing Division: NY

"The Ugly Vegetables" by Grace Lin. Text and illustrations copyright © 1999 by Grace Lin. Reprinted by permission of Charlesbridge Publishing.

ILLUSTRATIONS

Cover Illustration: Lisa Falkenstern

8–9: Diane Greenseid. 10–37: Julie Paschkis. 44–45: Diane Greenseid. 46–71: Peggy Rathmann. 74: Robert Schuster. 114: Richard Hewitt. 116–117: Jo Parry. 122–123: Bernard Adnet. 124–155: Joe Cepeda. 162: Pam Thompson. 164–165: Cindy Revell. 176–201: Eric Carle. 204: Daniel Del Valle. 210–233: Grace Lin. 238: Jenny Vainisi. 243: Grace Lin. 254–255: Marisol Sarrazin. 256–279: Holly Keller. 281–283: Andrea Tachiera. 284: Daniel Del Valle. 290–309: Ted Rand. 310: (bc) Ted Rand, (br) Wendell Minor. 311: Ted Rand. 317–319: Daniel Del Valle. 321: Greg Harris. 332–355: Barbara Bash. 360: Jenny Vainisi. 390–391: Rex Barron. 462–463: Deborah Melmon.

PHOTOGRAPHY

All Photographs are by Ken Karp for Macmillan/McGraw-Hill (MMH) except as noted below:

Inside Front Cover and back cover: Creatas/PunchStock. v: (t) Jupiter Images/Comstock Images; (b) Richard Hewett . vii: Maria Stenzel & Mark O. Thiessen/National Geographic Image Collection. viii: (b) Courtesy of Peter Arnold, Inc. Wildlife Pictures. ix: (t) Barbara Stitzer/Photo Edit; (b) Keith Kent/Science Photo Library/Photo Researchers. 2-3: A. Ramey / Photo Edit. 3: Jeff Greenberg/AGE Fotostock. 4: Mark Karrass. 5: ASSOCIATED PRESS. 6-7: Corbis/PunchStock. 36: (t) Courtesy of Won-Ldy Paye; (b) Courtesy of Julie Paschkis. 38-39: Comstock/PunchStock. 40: Tom Grill/Corbis. 41: Larry Bones/AGE Fotostock. 42-43: Jim Craigmyle/CORBIS. 70: Courtesy of Peggy Rathmann. 72: Kathy McLaughlin/The Image Works, Inc. 73: (t) Geri Engberg/The Image Works, Inc.; (b) Richard Hutchings/Photo Edit Inc. 74: Photodisc Green/Getty Images, Inc. 75: Michael Newman/Photo Edit Inc. 76: David Nagel/Allsport Concepts/Getty Images, Inc. 77: (t) Alaska Stock LLC/Alamy; (c) Ablestock/Hemera Technologies/Alamy. 78-79: Jupiter Images/Comstock Images. 80: (t) Keith Brofsky/Photodisc/Getty Images; (b) Suzanne Dunn/The Image Works. 81: Pete Saloutos/Corbis. 82: Ryan McVay/Photodisc/Getty Images. 83-85: Adamsmith/Taxi/Getty Images. 86: CORBIS. 88: Ryan McVay/Photodisc/Getty Images. 89: (l) Ryan McVay / Getty Images; (r) C Squared Studios/Getty Images; (bkgd) Bet Noire/Shutterstock. 90-91: Silver Image Photo Agency. 92: Tony Savino/ The Image Works, Inc. 94-115: Richard Hewett. 114: (t) Courtesy of Joan Hewett ; (b) Courtesy of Richard Hewett . 118: Lori Adamski-Peek /Jupiter Images. 119: Larime Photo/Dembinsky Photo Associates. 120-121: Aflo Foto Agency / Alamy. 154: Susan Werner. 154-155: Wetzel & Company. 156-157: Masterfile. 158: (tl) Simon Smith/DK Images; (tc) Rachel Epstein/Photo Edit Inc.; (tr) Andy Crawford/DK Images; (b) Jose Luis Pelaez, Inc./ CORBIS. 160: Rubberball/Alamy. 161: Rachel Epstein/Photo Edit Inc. 168-169: R. Ian Lloyd/Masterfile. 169: Ralph A. Clevenger/CORBIS. 170: David C Tomlinson/Getty Images. 171: Image A-08775 courtesy of Royal BC Museum, BC Archives. 172-173: Anthony Arendt / Alamy. 174: Masterfile Royalty Free. 175: Douglas Peebles/Corbis. 200: John Dolan. 202-203: MMH. 204: Laura Dwight/Photo Edit Inc. 205: C Squared Studios/Photodisc Green/Getty Images, Inc. 206-207: Blend Images/ PunchStock . 208: John A. Rizzo/Getty Images, Inc. 208-209: David Young-Wolff/Photo Edit Inc. 209: Jose Luis Pelaez, Inc./CORBIS. 232: Courtesy of Grace Lin. 234: (br) colinspics / Alamy; (bl) Jacques Cornell for MMH. 235: (t) Joe Sohm/Visions of America/Alamy; (b) Kevin Schafer / Alamy. 236: Jupiter Images. 237: Stockbyte/PunchStock. 238: Masterfile Royalty Free. 239: (tl) Picture Arts/CORBIS; (tc) Royalty-Free/CORBIS. 240-241: Maria Stenzel & Mark O. Thiessen/National Geographic Image Collection. 242: Norbert Wu. 243: REUTERS/Marcos Brindicci/Newscom. 245: (bl) Edward Degginger/Bruce Coleman Inc.; (br) Millard H. Sharp/Photo Researchers. 246: Mike Hettwer/National Geographic Image Collection. 247: REUTERS/Will Burgess/Newscom. 248: Courtesy David Krause/Madagascar Ankizy Fund. 250: Ross Whitaker/ The Image Bank/Getty Images. 251: (bl) Ryan McVay / Getty Images; (tr) PhotoLink/Getty Images; (br) C Squared Studios/Getty Images; (bkgd) Bet Noire/Shutterstock. 252-253: Martin Harvey/Gallo Images/CORBIS. 278: Courtesy of Holly Keller. 280: Frank Greenway/DK Images. 281: NHPA/Stephen Dalton. 284: Michael Newman/Photo Edit Inc. 285: Patricia Doyle/Photographer's Choice/Getty Images, Inc. 286-287: JEFFREY L. ROTMAN/Getty Images. 288: Bryan & Cherry Alexander Photography/Alamy. 288-289: Charlie Munsey/CORBIS. 289: Robert van der Hilst/Corbis. 310: (t) Courtesy of Jean Craighead George; (b) Courtesy of Ted Rand. 312-313: Stone/Getty Images, Inc. 313: David A. Northcott/CORBIS. 314: Jeff Lepore/Photo Researchers, Inc. 315: Tom Brakefield/CORBIS. 316: Richard Hutchings/Photo Edit Inc. 320: Scott Camazine / Photo Researchers, Inc. 320-321: John Pontier/ Animals Animals/Earth Scenes. 321: Daemon Becker. 324-325: Glow Images/Alamy. 325: Nicholas Parfitt /Getty Images. 326: F. Lukasseck/ Masterfile. 327: CORBIS. 328-329: Theo Allofs/CORBIS. 330: Vince Streano/CORBIS. 330-331: Norbert Rosing/National Geographic/Getty Images, Inc. 331: Ariel Skelley/CORBIS. 354: (t) Courtesy of April Pulley Sayre; (b) Courtesy of Barbara Bash. 356: Stan Osolinski/Dembinsky Photo Associates. 357: (t) Joe McDonald/CORBIS; (b) David Muench/ CORBIS. 358: George H. H. Huey/CORBIS. 359: (br) Daril Gulin/Dembinsky Photo Associates; (bl) Bill Lea/Dembinsky Photo Associates.

486

Acknowledgments

360: Photodisc Green/Getty Images, Inc. 361: Beth Davidow/Getty Images. 362-363: MedioImages/SuperStock. 364-365: Lee Cates/Getty Images, Inc. 365: Craig Tuttle/CORBIS. 366-367: Courtesy of Peter Arnold, Inc. Wildlife Pictures. 368-369: Peter Weimann/Animals Animals. 370-371: Ralph Reinhold/Animals Animals. 372: Gerard Lacz/Animals Animals. 372-373: Tim Fitzharris/Minden Pictures. 374: Frans Lanting. 375: Robert Winslow/Animals Animals. 376-377: The Nation Audubon Society Collection/Photo. Researchers/Mitch Reardon. 378-379: Gunter Ziesler/Peter Arnold. 380: Frans Lanting.381: The National Audubon Society Collection/Photo Researchers/Gregory Ochocki. 382-383: The National Audubon Society/Photo Researchers Allan Power. 384-385: Mike Severns/Getty Images. 386: The National Audubon Society/Photo Researchers/Mark Phillips. 387: Frans Lanting/Minden Pictures. 388: (tl) Frans Lanting; (tr) Courtesy of April Pulley Sayre. 389: Peter Weimann/Animals Animals/Earth Scenes. 392: Ross Whitaker/The Image Bank/Getty Images, Inc. 393: Tim Davis/Stone/Getty Images, Inc. 394-395: Barbara Stitzer/Photo Edit. 396: (t) Gloria H. Chomica / Masterfile; (b) Jim Brandenburg/Minden Pictures; (inset) Judy Griesedieck. 397: ZSSD/Minden Pictures. 398-399: Corbis. 399: (t) Walter Bibikow/The Image Bank/Getty Images; (c) Felicia Martinez/Photo Edit; (b) Photodisc/Getty Images. 400: (t) Comstock Images /Alamy; (c) Karl Weatherly/Corbis; (bc) Mark Gibson/Index Stock Imagery; (bl) Hank Morgan/Photo Researchers. 400-401: Courtesy Landscape Structures Inc. 401: Arthur Tilley/Taxi/Getty Images. 402: Marko Kokic/International Federation of Red Cross and Red Crescent Societies. 404: Ryan McVay/Photodisc/Getty Images. 405: (b) Gabe Palmer / Alamy; (t) PhotoLink/Getty Images; (bkgd) Bet Noire/Shutterstock. 406-407: Warren Faidley/Weatherstock.com. 408: Ellen Ozier/Reuters/CORBIS. 408-409: (c) Ron Sanford/CORBIS. 409: Mark J. Thomas/Dembinski Photo Associates. 410-411: Keith Kent/Science Photo Library/Photo Researchers, Inc. 412-413: George Post/Science Photo Library/Photo Researchers, Inc. 413: Jim Reed/ Photo Researchers, Inc. 414-415: Kent Wood/Science Source/Photo Researchers, Inc. 416-417: Kul Bhatia/Photo Researchers, Inc. 418-419: NOAA Central Library, OAR/ERL/National Severe Storms Labratory(NSSL). 419: Howard Bluestein/Photo Researchers, Inc. 420: Nancie Battaglia/ Nancie Battaglia Photography. 420-421: Science VU/Visuals Unlimited. 422-423: Bettmann/CORBIS. 423: Paul Buck/AFP/Getty Images, Inc. 426: NOAA,NESDIS, Science Source/Photo Researchers, Inc. 426-427: Annie Griffiths Belt/National Geographic Image Collection. 428: Joel Sartore/National Geographic Image Collection. 428-429: James L. Amos/CORBIS. 430: AP-Wide World Photos. 430-431: Howard Bluestein/ Photo Researchers, Inc. 432: Courtesy of Seymour Simon. 432-433: George Post/Science Photo Library/Photo Researchers, Inc. 433: Kent Wood/Science Source/Photo Researchers, Inc. 434-435: Bettmannn/ CORBIS. 436: Laura Dwight/Photo Edit Inc. 437: Richard Hutchings/ Photo Edit Inc. 438-439: Roger Ressmeyer/CORBIS. 456: (t) Courtesy of Joseph Bruchac; (b) Courtesy of Stefano Vitale. 458: Courtesy of Joseph Bruchac. 460: Stephen Marks/The Image Bank/Getty Images, Inc. 461: Michael Newman/Photo Edit Inc. 464: Richard T. Nowitz/CORBIS. 465: (t) Courtesy of Tom and Anne Moore. 468: (br) Peter Griffith/Masterfile; (bl) Stone/Getty Images, Inc. 469: (t) Mark Tomalty/Masterfile; (b) Bruce Heinemann/Getty Images. 470: Mira / Alamy. 471: (c) Digital Vision Ltd.; (b) Mark Tomalty/Masterfile. 472: Bruce Heinemann/Getty Images. 473: Jeff Greenberg/AGE Fotostock. 474: (b) David Buffington/Getty Images; (c) Paul A. Souders/CORBIS. 475: Peter Griffith/Masterfile. 476: E. Krenkel/ Zefa/Masterfile. 477: Spencer Grant/Photo Edit Inc. 478: (c): Stone/Getty Images, Inc.; (b) Paul Barton/CORBIS. 479: Eric and David Hosking/ CORBIS. 480: (tl) Gary Smith/AGE Fotostock; (tr) T. Allofs/Zefa/Masterfile. 481: (c) Kevin Dodge/Masterfile; (b) Brand X Pictures/Picturequest. 482: Richard Hutchings/Workbookstock. 483: Randy Faris/CORBIS. 484: (t) Ian Shaw / Alamy; (b) Dale Wilson/Masterfile. 485: Martin Rugner/AGE Fotostock. . California Standards 1-4: Medioimages/PunchStock

Reading/Language Arts
CA California Standards
Grade 2

READING

1.0 Word Analysis, Fluency, and Systematic Vocabulary Development
Students understand the basic features of reading. They select letter patterns and know how to translate them into spoken language by using phonics, syllabication, and word parts. They apply this knowledge to achieve fluent oral and silent reading.

Decoding and Word Recognition

1.1 Recognize and use knowledge of spelling patterns (e.g., diphthongs, special vowel spellings) when reading.

1.2 Apply knowledge of basic syllabication rules when reading (e.g., vowel-consonant-vowel = *su/per;* vowel-consonant/consonant-vowel = *sup/per*).

1.3 Decode two-syllable nonsense words and regular multisyllable words.

1.4 Recognize common abbreviations (e.g., *Jan., Sun., Mr., St.*).

1.5 Identify and correctly use regular plurals (e.g., *-s, -es, -ies*) and irregular plurals (e.g., *fly/ flies, wife/ wives*).

1.6 Read aloud fluently and accurately and with appropriate intonation and expression.

Vocabulary and Concept Development

1.7 Understand and explain common antonyms and synonyms.

1.8 Use knowledge of individual words in unknown compound words to predict their meaning.

1.9 Know the meaning of simple prefixes and suffixes (e.g., *over-, un-, -ing, -ly*).

1.10 Identify simple multiple-meaning words.

2.0 Reading Comprehension Students read and understand grade-level-appropriate material. They draw upon a variety of comprehension strategies as needed (e.g., generating and responding to essential questions, making predictions, comparing information from several sources). The selections in *Recommended Literature, Kindergarten Through Grade Twelve* illustrate the quality and complexity of the materials to be read by students. In addition to their regular school reading, by grade four, students read one-half million words annually, including a good representation of grade-level-appropriate narrative and expository text (e.g., classic and contemporary literature, magazines, newspapers, online information). In grade two, students continue to make progress toward this goal.

READING (continued)

Structural Features of Informational Materials

2.1	Use titles, tables of contents, and chapter headings to locate information in expository test.

Comprehension and Analysis of Grade-Level-Appropriate Text

2.2	State the purpose in reading (i. e., tell what information is sought).
2.3	Use knowledge of the author's purpose(s) to comprehend informational text.
2.4	Ask clarifying questions about essential textual elements of exposition (e.g., *why, what if, how*).
2.5	Restate facts and details in the text to clarify and organize ideas.
2.6	Recognize cause-and-effect relationships in a text.
2.7	Interpret information from diagrams, charts, and graphs.
2.8	Follow two-step written instructions.

3.0 Literary Response and Analysis Students read and respond to a wide variety of significant works of children's literature. They distinguish between the structural features of the text and the literary terms or elements (e.g., theme, plot, setting, characters). The selections in *Recommended Literature, Kindergarten Through Grade Twelve* illustrate the quality and complexity of the materials to be read by students.

Narrative Analysis of Grade-Level-Appropriate Text

3.1	Compare and contrast plots, settings, and characters presented by different authors.
3.2	Generate alternative endings to plots and identify the reason or reasons for, and the impact of, the alternatives.
3.3	Compare and contrast different versions of the same stories that reflect different cultures.
3.4	Identify the use of rhythm, rhyme, and alliteration in poetry.

WRITING

1.0 Writing Strategies Students write clear and coherent sentences and paragraphs that develop a central idea. Their writing shows they consider the audience and purpose. Students progress through the stages of the writing process (e.g., prewriting, drafting, revising, editing successive versions).

Organization and Focus

1.1	Group related ideas and maintain a consistent focus.

Penmanship

1.2	Create readable documents with legible handwriting.

Research

1.3   Understand the purposes of various reference materials (e.g., dictionary, thesaurus, atlas).

Evaluation and Revision

1.4   Revise original drafts to improve sequence and provide more descriptive detail.

2.0 Writing Applications (Genres and Their Characteristics) Students write compositions that describe and explain familiar objects, events, and experiences. Student writing demonstrates a command of standard American English and the drafting, research, and organizational strategies outlined in Writing Standard 1.0.

Using the writing strategies of grade two outlined in Writing Standard 1.0, students:

2.1   Write brief narratives based on their experiences:
       a. Move through a logical sequence of events.
       b. Describe the setting, characters, objects, and events in detail.

2.2   Write a friendly letter complete with the date, salutation, body, closing, and signature.

WRITTEN AND ORAL ENGLISH LANGUAGE CONVENTIONS

The standards for written and oral English language conventions have been placed between those for writing and for listening and speaking because these conventions are essential to both sets of skills.

1.0 Written and Oral English Language Conventions Students write and speak with a command of standard English conventions appropriate to this grade level.

Sentence Structure

1.1   Distinguish between complete and incomplete sentences.

1.2   Recognize and use the correct word order in written sentences.

Grammar

1.3   Identify and correctly use various parts of speech, including nouns and verbs, in writing and speaking.

Punctuation

1.4   Use commas in the greeting and closure of a letter and with dates and items in a series.

1.5   Use quotation marks correctly.

Capitalization

1.6   Capitalize all proper nouns, words at the beginning of sentences and greetings, months and days of the week, and titles and initials of people.

WRITTEN AND ORAL ENGLISH LANGUAGE CONVENTIONS
(continued)

Spelling

1.7	Spell frequently used, irregular words correctly (e.g., *was, were, says, said, who, what, why*).
1.8	Spell basic short-vowel, long-vowel, *r-* controlled, and consonant-blend patterens correctly.

LISTENING AND SPEAKING

1.0 Listening and Speaking Strategies Students listen critically and respond appropriately to oral communication. They speak in a manner that guides the listener to understand important ideas by using proper phrasing, pitch, and modulation.

Comprehension

1.1	Determine the purpose or purposes of listening (e.g., to obtain information, to solve problems, for enjoyment).
1.2	Ask for clarification and explanation of stories and ideas.
1.3	Paraphrase information that has been shared orally by others.
1.4	Give and follow three- and four-step oral directions.

Organization and Delivery of Oral Communication

1.5	Organize presentations to maintain a clear focus.
1.6	Speak clearly and at an appropriate pace for the type of communication (e.g., informal discussion, report to class).
1.7	Recount experiences in a logical sequence.
1.8	Retell stories, including characters, setting, and plot.
1.9	Report on a topic with supportive facts and details.

2.0 Speaking Applications (Genres and Their Characteristics) Students deliver brief recitations and oral presentations about familiar experiences or interests that are organized around a coherent thesis statement. Student speaking demonstrates a command of standard American English and the organizational and delivery strategies outlined in Listening and Speaking Standard 1.0.

Using the speaking strategies of grade two outlined in Listening and Speaking Standard 1.0, students:

2.1	Recount experiences or present stories: a. Move through a logical sequence of events. b. Describe story elements (e.g., characters, plot, setting).
2.2	Report on a topic with facts and details, drawing from several sources of information.